THE GREAT CHICAGO FIRE OF 1871

GREAT HISTORIC DISASTERS

GREAT HISTORIC DISASTERS

THE
GREAT CHICAGO FIRE
OF 1871

PAUL BENNIE

CHELSEA HOUSE
PUBLISHERS
An imprint of Infobase Publishing

THE GREAT CHICAGO FIRE OF 1871

Copyright © 2008 by Infobase Publishing

Chelsea House
An imprint of Infobase Publishing
132 West 31st Street
New York NY 10001

Library of Congress Cataloging-in-Publication Data
Bennie, Paul.
The great Chicago fire of 1871/Paul Bennie.
  p. cm.—(Great historic disasters)
Includes bibliographical references and index.
ISBN: 978-0-7910-9638-3 (hardcover)
1. Great Fire, Chicago, Ill., 1871—Juvenile literature. 2. Fires—Illinois—Chicago—History—19th Century— Juvenile literature. 3. Chicago (Ill.)—History—To 1875— Juvenile literature. I. Title.
F548.42.B46 2008
977.3'041—dc22   2007036550

Chelsea House books are available at special discounts when purchased in bulk quantities for businesses, associations, institutions, or sales promotions. Please call our Special Sales Department in New York at (212) 967-8800 or (800) 322-8755.

You can find Chelsea House on the World Wide Web
at http://www.chelseahouse.com

Text design by Annie O'Donnell
Cover design by Ben Peterson

Printed in the United States of America

Bang KT 10 9 8 7 6 5 4 3 2 1

This book is printed on acid-free paper.

All links and Web addresses were checked and verified to be correct at the time of publication. Because of the dynamic nature of the Web, some addresses and links may have changed since publication and may no longer be valid.

Contents

Introduction:
A National Event

On the evening of October 7, 1871, a famous author and world traveler named George Francis Train was giving a lecture in Chicago when he suddenly stopped, overcome by an eerie premonition, or warning. Looking solemnly out at the packed auditorium, he said, "This is the last public address that will be delivered within these walls! A terrible calamity is impending over the city of Chicago! More I cannot say; more I dare not utter."

Within 24 hours of this peculiar outburst, two fires broke out within one hour of each other on the shore of Lake Michigan. One was the Peshtigo Fire, a 100-foot-high fireball that rolled like a boulder through a lumber town in Wisconsin, instantly killing 2,000 people and securing its place as the deadliest fire in the history of America. The other was the Great Chicago Fire, which had its humble origins in a cow barn, then swept like a fever through the heart of the city, destroying thousands of buildings, killing 300 people, and leaving 100,000 homeless. Both were deeply tragic events, but it seems curious, these many years later, that the Great Chicago Fire monopolized, or dominated, the public interest, when a simultaneous firestorm claimed six times as many lives. In her book *Smoldering City*, Karen Sawislak suggests that the Great Chicago Fire captured everyone's imagination precisely because it took place in a city. That is, in the years before the turn of the century, industrialization, technology, and the growth of the modern city were sensational topics with the power to fascinate and horrify. People could not read enough about the wonders and horrors of the city: On the one hand, there were exciting new inventions such as trolley cars, tall buildings, and factories with assembly lines; and on the other, there were grimy streets, slums, gambling, and murder. Perhaps more than any other city in the country, Chicago seemed to embody this Jekyll-and-Hyde nature. It was a potent mix of the rich and poor, the native born and immigrant, the traditional and modern, the horse cart and train. Having grown from a muddy settlement to a great metropolis in less than half a century, Chicago seemed like a dangerous chemistry experiment about to explode, and people were hungry for news of its every development.

It was these very growing pains that led to the horror of October 8, 1871. Chicago had developed too quickly and haphazardly, with flammable wooden planks as its building material of choice. Its fire department was under-equipped, and its citizens had grown complacent, or unconcerned, about the risk of fire. Then, beginning in late summer, the city suffered a prolonged drought that dried out all its wooden buildings. By autumn, small fires were breaking out all over town. When a blaze flared up in Mrs. O'Leary's barn, it was only a matter of hours before the flames raged out of control. The streets became a crazed parade of fleeing residents, and the waterways became a knot of burning boats. By the time the inferno had exhausted itself, one-third of the city was completely destroyed, with property damages totaling $200 million, and emotional damages that cannot be reckoned.

Even as these events were unfolding, the telegraph wires were humming with the news. In New York, Boston, and other

The Great Chicago Fire blazed through Chicago, using the city's wooden sidewalks and buildings as the fuel for what was to become one of the most destructive fires in U.S. history.

major cities, crowds stood about the telegraph offices and lined up at the newspaper outlets, which provided around-the-clock dispatches. Many who heard the news regarded Chicago as a modern-day Gomorrah, a wicked city being punished by a wrathful God. Others rushed to send relief aid, seeing the fire as an opportunity to show the unity of the United States after the Civil War. But whatever the response, there is no mistaking the country's preoccupation with the fate of the city or the role the telegraph played in pulling everyone together. In fact, it was the lack of telegraph offices in Peshtigo that helped ensure that town's obscurity: There was only a single telegraph line in the little village, and it burned immediately after the firestorm began.

Ultimately, America's love affair with the tale of the "Great Fire" had as much to do with rebirth as destruction. The city rebuilt itself with astonishing speed, the first shipment of lumber arriving even before the flames were out. The country drew inspiration from the city's determination and resilience, and from the excitement of a slate wiped clean. When a talented group of architects poured into Chicago to help it rebuild in style, the nation shared in the feeling of triumph. Rows of steel and glass skyscrapers, the beacons of a new century, seemed to spring up overnight. By the time of the Chicago World's Fair in 1893, the city was truly a new creation, ready for its unveiling to millions of fairgoers. It was clear that Chicago, like the band of states so recently torn by the Civil War, had survived its painful adolescence and crossed into adulthood.

1 City in a Hurry

Chicago grew up fast. In fact, few American cities have shown such a sudden, meteoric rise. In 1833, the year of its founding, Chicago consisted of a government fort and about 150 residents living in wooden cabins on a patch of soggy marshland. There were no gaslights, no sewage system, and no running water. The mud was so thick that wagons got stuck in it up to their axles, and at night, starving wolves roamed the streets for food. Less than 40 years later, in 1871, the population had swollen to a whopping 334,000, making Chicago the largest city in the West, and the fourth largest in the nation. It now had elegant hotels, theaters, and marble-faced department stores. In fact, it had about 60,000 buildings, spread across 36 square miles. America's major railroad lines converged in its rail yards, and the city's harbor welcomed more ships than the ports of New York; Philadelphia; Baltimore; San Francisco; Charleston, South Carolina; and Mobile, Alabama, combined. How could such a ragged frontier settlement grow, in such a short period of time, to become the grandest city of the West? The answer can be given in one word: location.

THE GREAT WATERWAYS

Chicago sits on the rim of the greatest inland waterway on Earth, the Great Lakes–St. Lawrence system. This massive water system starts with the five Great Lakes, which link together like a single river that runs along the northernmost edges of eight American states, and continues eastward on the St. Lawrence River all the way to the Atlantic Ocean. From its purchase on the southwestern rim of Lake Michigan, Chicago was in a perfect location to receive timber and iron from the northern forests and ore mines. Moreover, through the Erie Canal, it could receive ships from as far east as New York—or even Europe. And like New York, Chicago had a natural inlet, the Chicago River, which ran from the lake into the heart of the city. This gentle river allowed ships to leave the often stormy lake and take shelter while loading and unloading their goods.

Even with all of these gifts, Chicago might never have developed into more than a rough community of Indians and fur traders. But the little prairie town had been given one more geographical advantage. It was also very close to the *second* greatest water system in North America, the Mississippi River System, which runs south from Minnesota to the Gulf of Mexico. For hundreds of years, American Indians had taken advantage of the nearness of the two mighty water systems. They would canoe to the tip of Lake Michigan, then carry their canoes over a land route, or portage, to rivers running south into the Mississippi. By combining the Great Lakes and the Great River, the Indians could move in four directions across the plains. Unfortunately, the trip across the portage was grueling. The journey required several days, and the canoes had to be pulled through thick mud and prairie grass, while slimy bloodsuckers, flies, and mosquitoes attacked from all sides. It was impossible, under these conditions, to carry heavy cargo or transport large boats.

That was the situation in 1830 when the state planners of Illinois finally decided to do what explorers, traders, and land speculators had dreamed of since the seventeenth century.

Because of its prime location, Chicago was able to connect waterways to allow for the transportation of goods from the West to people who needed them in the East. In this illustration, ships load cargo at the Lake Michigan grain elevators, at a location that would become one of the United States' biggest and busiest cities.

They made plans to build a canal over the portage, finally connecting the St. Lawrence River, the Erie Canal, the Great Lakes, and all the branches of the Mississippi into one big web of water roads. And sitting at the point where all these routes converged was the little town of Chicago.

As Donald L. Miller explains in his epic history of Chicago, *City of the Century*, this was the realization of a long-standing dream. As long ago as 1674, the French explorer Louis Jolliet tried to convince the French government in Canada to build a canal over the portage. With such a canal, he predicted, the French could begin to control North America.

And in 1683, another French explorer, René-Robert Cavelier, sieur de La Salle, camped on the portage and wrote about it in his journal:

> [Through this] lowest point on the divide between the two great valleys of the St. Lawrence and the Mississippi . . . the boundless regions of the West must send their products to the East . . . This will be the gate of empire, this the seat of commerce. Everything invites to action. The typical man who will grow up here must be an enterprising man. Each day as he rises he will exclaim, "I act, I move, I push," and there will be spread before him a boundless horizon, an illimitable field of activity.

BLACK HAWK AND THE INDIAN "PROBLEM"

But before all these predictions about Chicago could come true, one remaining problem had to be solved. The land surrounding the portage—and indeed, much of the land in Illinois—was still occupied by Indian tribes. In 1832, the federal government took a decisive step to change this. Citing an earlier, disputed treaty, federal soldiers escorted Chief Black Hawk and his community of Sauk and Fox Indians across the Mississippi River into Iowa and warned them not to come back.

This did not sit well with Black Hawk, who had been a mighty warrior all his life. In his autobiography, Black Hawk describes how, at age 16, he first volunteered to go to war with his father against the Osage tribe:

> [I] was proud to have an opportunity to prove to [my father] that I was not an unworthy son, and that I had courage and bravery. It was not long before we met the enemy and a battle immediately ensued. Standing by my father's side, I saw him kill his antagonist and tear the scalp from off his head. Fired with valor and ambition, I rushed furiously

upon another and smote him to the earth with my toma-
hawk. I then ran my lance through his body, took off his
scalp and returned in triumph to my father. He said nothing
but looked well pleased. This was the first man I killed . . .
Our party then returned to the village and danced over the
scalps we had taken. This was the first time I was permitted
to join in a scalp dance.

As an adult, Black Hawk went on to conquer the Cherokee
and to fight the British in the War of 1812. But in 1832, when
his tribes were dispossessed, or deprived, of their lands, the
aging Black Hawk decided to try a different approach. He did
not want to use force to regain the homelands of his people.
Instead, he convinced his tribes to return across the Mississippi and peacefully resume farming. They would return
with old men and women and children, carrying seeds for
harvest, to prove they meant peace. By quietly planting their
crops instead of fighting, they would show that these fertile
plains were still their lands, just as they had been for hundreds of years, and the militia would leave them alone. This
tragic miscalculation led to the 15-week war known as the
Black Hawk War.

On the spring morning when Black Hawk and his tribe
returned to Illinois, the governor called out a group of militiamen to protect the state. The next night, about 400 of these
men were camped at White Rock Grove, drinking from a bar-
rel of whiskey. While the militiamen were having their party,
a small group of Black Hawk's men approached with a white
flag of truce, again declaring their peaceful intentions. But
the sight of the approaching Indians terrified the militiamen.
They panicked and fired at the flag bearers, killing two of
them instantly, then seized and killed two more. Minutes later,
Black Hawk sounded the war whoop. Rolling in anger across
the plains with 100 horsemen, he sent the militiamen into a
chaotic retreat, quickly killing 11 of them.

When the U.S. government decided that it needed to build a canal to connect the Mississippi River, Lake Michigan, and the St. Lawrence Canal, they worried that the local Native American population would pose a threat to their plans. Black Hawk *(left)* and his tribe, the Sauk, were moved to Iowa due, they were told, to a treaty dispute. He later returned with his tribe, sparking the Black Hawk War.

This would be the chief's final victory. In the ensuing, or following, weeks, the government mobilized 7,000 soldiers. The small band of Indian warriors, many of them half-starving or sick, had no chance against a force of this size. In the end, the Indians were forced into a retreat, but their progress was slowed by their sick, their elderly, and their children. At the Bad Axe River, the party was attempting to cross back into Iowa when the militia caught up with them. Historian Donald Miller describes the terrible slaughter that ensued:

Many of the victims were scalped by white soldiers, and some of those killed were women attempting to swim across the river with children on their backs. Those in

Black Hawk's band who made it to the west bank were pursued by the Sioux, the ancient enemies of the Fox and Sauk, and killed. Black Hawk surrendered, and he and his son, Whirling Thunder, were sent on a tour of the eastern states by President Jackson to witness the spread and the might of the nation they had attempted to defy.

After this defeat, the remaining tribes in Illinois were too dispirited to resist the inevitable pressure to sell their lands. In 1833, 6,000 Indians from the Potawatami, Chippewa, and Ottawa tribes formed a huge circle of tents around the tiny village of Chicago to negotiate with government agents for their final parcel of land, the 5 million acres around the portage. Donald Miller describes how the Indians attempted to slow the negotiations. "They went back to their encampments and delayed for well over a week . . . drinking great quantities of whiskey that ravenous traders sold them for the promise of [their] treaty money." In their depression, they drank, gambled with the traders, raced their ponies, and fought each other with knives. At night, they patrolled the village "screaming war chants and brandishing their tomahawks." In the end, though, when the soldiers fired their canons as a final warning, the Indian tribes were outgunned, and they knew it. They signed the treaty papers. In exchange for their ancestral lands, they were given a tract farther west, a piece of land the government had determined was "too poor for snakes to live on." They were also given $1 million in goods, but they had to give much of it back to pay for their food and whiskey.

CITY OF WOOD

This was the end of the road for the Great Lake Indian tribes, but it was only the beginning for Chicago. Even before the treaties were signed, the rasp of saws and banging of hammers could be heard throughout the village. On the promise of a new canal, land speculators had already begun to flood into the city from New York and to put up new buildings. From this point forward, the construction and excitement were almost nonstop. Mobs of capitalists, speculators, and developers jostled each other in the dusty streets, running manically from one land sale to another. Teams of men worked to drain squares of the swampy land, which then sold for hundreds of thousand of dollars. No matter how high the property values went, people still kept pouring in, hoping to make a fast buck on a land deal or get rich with a business venture. From the city of Buffalo, New York, alone, 250 wagons full of immigrants left for Chicago each day. These settlers were a special breed. Part cheerful optimist and part hustler, they had an itchy, restless energy that made things happen. They were the sort of people who said "I act, I move, I push," just as La Salle had predicted.

"All is astir here," wrote the popular writer Sara Jane Lippincott during a visit to the city. "There is no such thing as stagnation or rest. Lake-winds and prairie-winds keep the very air in commotion. You catch the contagion of activity and enterprise, and have wild dreams of beginning life again, and settling—no circulating, *whirling*—in Chicago, the rapids and wild eddies of business have such a powerful fascination for one."

The Illinois and Michigan Canal finally opened in 1848, the same year that construction began on the city's first railroad. This thundering, smoke-belching machine would soon eclipse the canal in importance. In fact, if the canal had turned Chicago from a swamp into a boomtown, it was the railroad that turned that boomtown into a metropolis. Once again, geography played a major part in this transformation. Because Lake Michigan dips deep into the continent, blocking the shortest route from east to west, railroads traveling across the country had to go around the lake and through the city. Soon, like the spokes in a wheel, all the country's major railroad lines converged on Chicago. The city quickly beat its closest rivals, St. Louis and Cincinnati, for control of the trade in the country's interior, and by the mid-1850s, it had become the world's greatest rail center. More railroads met at Chicago than anywhere else on Earth, earning the city the nickname "Big Junction." The trains even crisscrossed within the city, coating the streets with their black soot and scattering pedestrians and carriage horses at the unmarked crossings.

The new industries and trade routes complemented each other. For example, the railroads carried homesteaders to the prairies, where people sliced away the tallgrass, plowed the land, and planted seeds in what would prove to be the most fertile farmland on Earth. When the golden wheat was ready for harvest, a new invention called the reaper, built in Chicago, cut the harvesting time in half. The reaper was a horse-driven machine with back-and-forth blades. Thousands of the shiny red reapers were built at McCormick's Reaper Works in Chicago and delivered to the farms by train. When the golden harvest was ready, railroads carried the wheat to Chicago, where gigantic grain elevators, another Chicago invention, lifted it from the train beds and poured it into steamers bound for Canada and Buffalo. Trains also carried livestock—cattle, pigs, and sheep—from the farms to the slaughterhouses, and then away again as packaged beef, pork, and mutton. The slaughterhouses grew so big that an entire city was created just outside of Chicago to house and process the animals. This separate city had its own streets and sewage system, lighted pens that could house 120,000 animals, and even a cream-colored hotel for visiting cattlemen. Unfortunately, it also released a foul odor that drifted over the streets of Chicago and mingled with the choking clouds of smoke.

Perhaps the most important cargo carried by the trains, schooners, and steamships was wood. The region had no forests of its own, and the city's unprecedented growth required white pine from northern forests. Chicago's appetite for wood was enormous. As Donald Miller explains: "The Chicago harbor handled the largest lumber fleet in the world, was the largest

Raising Chicago

In the 1850s, a new sewage system was built in Chicago, and, in order to fit the new pipes beneath the existing streets and buildings, the entire grade of the city had to be raised as much as 10 feet. The city raised the streets, but building owners had to raise their own buildings. Even huge hotels and department stores were lifted, by placing hundreds of jack-screws beneath. Workers would turn the screws a little bit at a time, raising the structure just an inch or so, while bricklayers worked frantically to raise the foundation. Spectators and tourists often crowded around to watch.

market for forest products in the world, and had the world's largest lumberyard. Entire city blocks contained nothing but docks and yards with white pine heaped a dozen and more feet high. . . . By 1870, over two-hundred lumber boats were arriving in Chicago every twelve hours."

These endless piles of wood were used to build houses, bridges, sidewalks, even the streets themselves. In fact, wood seemed to be the perfect material for an instant city like Chicago. Everything could be erected quickly and cheaply. Unfortunately, since profit and haste were the main guiding principles, much of the construction was haphazard, shoddy, and crowded. And of course, as would soon become tragically clear, a wooden city is also dangerously vulnerable to flames.

In the meantime, an invention called the balloon frame helped speed the construction. The balloon frame was a faster, cheaper way to build wood houses, and Chicago was the first city to use it widely. Before the balloon frame, houses were built using a mortise-and-tenon method. This was a laborious process in which holes and tongues were cut into heavy beams to fit them together. In balloon frame construction, pine boards were simply nailed together to make a light frame, which was then covered with siding to form walls. This technique, which is still the main construction method used in America today, gained its name from the perceived flimsiness of the houses it produced, which seemed at risk of blowing away like balloons in the wind.

In many of the poorer neighborhoods of the city, pine frame cottages and shanties were packed two to a lot, with one house facing the street and the other hidden behind it. One observer described the houses in Conley's Patch, an impoverished, crime-ridden district, as the "most rickety, one-sided, leaning

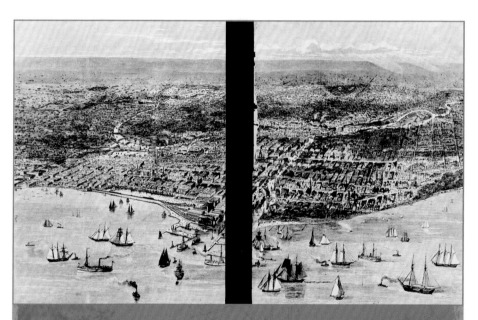

This illustration, rendered to look like a stereoscopic image, shows Chicago before it was consumed by the Great Fire. As the city grew, wagons full of immigrants arrived, and the addition of the railroad brought more people. Six years after the completion of the canal, Chicago's population had tripled.

forward, propped up, tumbled-down, sinking fast, low-roofed and miserable shanties." Wedged between the homes like powder kegs were little barns and sheds filled with hay, coal, and wood shavings for cooking. Thrown into this jumble were small factories and warehouses filled with lumber to make wagons, chairs, pianos, and boats. And outside the factories sat mountains of coal for the steam-fueled boilers. Historian Robert Cromie, in his classic account *The Great Chicago Fire*, puts it succinctly: "It might be said, with considerable justice, that Chicago specialized in the production, handling, and storage of combustible goods."

To prevent the spread of these wooden warrens, the city had designated special areas where it was illegal to build balloon frame houses, but these rules were thought to interfere with free enterprise and private property, and builders ignored them. As historian Edgar Lee Masters wrote 50 years after the fire: "Reckless moneyed interests . . . continued to build the city in this fashion. They saw no reason for pulling down wooden buildings and erecting in their stead buildings of brick or stone, for that took away from the income of property. The menace of such buildings to the city was subordinated to the ambition to get richer."

In all, approximately two-thirds of the city's buildings were made of wood. There were also buildings of brick, stone, and marble, but many of these were secretly built with white pine frames, then faced with a thin layer of some more impressive building material. In part, this was because Chicago had an image problem. The city's architects knew that the acres of rickety wooden structures were not as grand as the magnificent avenues of old European cities or as imposing as the heavy brownstones lining the streets of New York, and to compensate, they sometimes built ostentatious buildings that pretended to be what they were not. Church steeples that appeared to be stone might really be wooden scaffolding wrapped with tin, and painted to look like masonry. Brick buildings hundreds of feet high were sometimes no thicker than a single brick, and their walls repeatedly toppled over into the streets. Decorating these sham buildings were heavy marble columns and massive stone sculptures that were really just more painted wood and putty (and that were also known to plunge to the streets in a stiff wind).

Connecting all these buildings like a golden fuse were miles of wooden streets and sidewalks. The wooden streets were covered with heavy pine blocks instead of bricks or cobblestones. The wooden sidewalks were built as an unusual solution to the mud problem. After rain or snow, the streets of Chicago turned into big, sloppy mud holes, and in order to keep pedestrians from slogging through this mess, runners were laid down like train tracks, and pine planks were laid across them. These sidewalks were often raised to keep them well above the mud, often as much as five to seven feet—high enough that a person could walk upright beneath them. Of course, if there was room for people to walk along these "underground" passages, then the oxygen needed to fuel a fire could race through as well. By sucking up oxygen and creating a vacuum, a fire could pull thousands of cubic feet of air through these tunnels, stoking the flames from beneath like the air in a giant bellows.

2 Drought and Blaze

I n 1871, Chicago was the fastest-growing city in America, but slapdash, or haphazard, wooden construction had imperiled it to an invisible enemy. A single spark from a tossed-down cigar or unattended candle could ignite a fire that would rage unchecked. Chicagoans were not entirely blind to the threat. Only one month before the Great Fire, the *Tribune*, the city's largest newspaper, had warned Chicagoans that the buildings downtown were mere "firetraps pleasing to the eye" and nothing more than "shams and shingles."

THE LULL AND HOLMES FIRE

October 1871 was another dry month in Chicago. The last decent rains had fallen over three months ago, and now the wells were dry, the grass was brown, and the tar roofs simmered and bubbled in the sun. Each day, dry winds from the overheated prairies blew into the city and parched all the buildings. This was a dangerous condition for a town built of white pine. From the wooden fences marking the boundaries of every property to the sheds filled with hay and pine shavings, everything in Chicago had grown brittle as kindling under the sweltering sun.

Under dry conditions such as these, anything might start a fire, and just about everything did. Boys playing with matches accidentally set their house on fire. A spark flew from the torch of a roof repairman and started a church burning. Old rags and papers suddenly burst into flame in a basement. Sparks rose from a chimney, landed on a hotel and burned it to the ground. A kerosene lamp exploded and started a fire. Two horses died in an inferno in a barn, and a railroad car mysteriously burst into flames. In just the first seven days of October, there were a total of 28 fires in Chicago. The firemen were exhausted, racing their horse-drawn steamers from blaze to blaze, pushing their way past the crowds of gawkers in the streets. They did not have enough time to sleep or to repair their equipment. No sooner was one fire conquered than the courthouse bell rang again, signaling the location of another.

And then, on Saturday, October 7, less than 24 hours before the start of the most infamous fire in American history, a blaze at the Lull and Holmes Planing Mill sapped the final strength of the firefighters. The planing mill was a woodworking factory in the West Side of Chicago, nestled in among frame houses, a paper-box company, and coal yards. Seven million feet of wood were stacked in lumberyards in the surrounding neighborhood. The mill caught fire around 11:00 P.M.—no one was ever sure why—and the flames quickly jumped to other buildings. A strong wind drove the fire north, then changed direction and drove it southwest. The piles of lumber caught fire and helped scatter the flames like quicksilver; in only 20 minutes, four city blocks were ablaze. Three alarms were sounded—the code for a fire out of control—and all the city's firemen and engines roused themselves again.

Fires in Chicago were cheap entertainment. When the skies lit up with the rose glow of flames, people poured from their houses like a bell had rung at a free boxing match. The Lull and Holmes fire was the largest conflagration yet, and thousands took to the streets to watch it. They blocked traffic and interfered with the firefighters, and the police had to force them off the Adams Street Bridge. All the rooftops were filled with spectators, too. One hundred and fifty people crowded onto the roof of a shed, causing it to collapse and pitching them into the street. A deputy police commissioner ordered his men to arrest onlookers who got in the way, but as historian Robert Cromie says, "The threat was totally ineffectual. Such a mass arrest would have filled every jail in town, with prisoners left over."

Sometimes the bystanders made themselves useful by assisting the beleaguered fire department. In the case of the Lull and Holmes fire, the firemen had their hands full on

The lumber district of Chicago *(above)* provided the wood that builders and architects used to construct most of Chicago's buildings. Because of its availability, wood was used for housing, municipal buildings, and even sidewalks, making Chicago more susceptible to fires.

Adams Street, preventing the blaze from spreading north, and they did not have the manpower to protect the river, with its wooden bridges, wooden ships, and wooden train cars lined up on tracks along the water. The spectators sprung into action to save a group of railroad freight and passenger buildings, tearing down sheds that lay between the fire and the bigger buildings, so the flames would run out of fuel. Then, braving the intense heat, these amateur firefighters managed to roll the train cars safely out of the way. At a lumberyard on the river-bank, a handful of men were trying to fight the flames, but the advancing fire forced them back until they were trapped between the fire and the water. Using planks from the lumberyard to keep them afloat, the men paddled to safety on the opposite shore.

Meanwhile the fire department was putting up a heroic fight. They had drawn a line at Adams Street, determined the fire would not cross over. They hooked up 12 hoses and completely flooded the burning area, getting as close as humanly possible to the blistering heat, pushing back against the fire and taking their territory inch by inch. When their lungs were too seared to breathe, they dropped back a few feet and caught their breath, only to charge forward again. The bystanders watched in awed silence, while burning chunks of wood rained from the sky at their feet, and the horses reared and whinnied in terror.

On the opposite side of the street, a saloon owner named Daniel Quirk watched the inferno roll up the street, building by building, and concluded that his saloon would be one of the next to go. Deciding to go out with style, he threw open his bar to the crowds, offering free drinks and cigars as concessions for the fiery show. The crowd filled the building eagerly, helping themselves to the finest whiskey and wine before the fire could take everything for itself. Then they repaid Daniel Quirk for his generosity. Using portable fire extinguishers, they doused the outside of his saloon with water. This kept the walls from catching fire amid the swirl of sparks and cinders, and finally saved the little building.

The firemen and citizens did indeed stop the advance of the fire across Adams Street. "It was not accident, nor extraneous influence, that checked the fire here, but calm, deliberate, intelligent heroism," writes historian Alfred T. Andreas. Here and on other fronts, the department fought all night and much of Sunday afternoon—17 hours in total. When the blaze was finally snuffed out, all that remained of four city blocks were smoldering mounds of coal and ash. The firefighters went home, stripped off their blackened fire suits, and collapsed into bed, their eyelids nearly swollen shut from the smoke and stinging cinders. Many of them had smoke poisoning. Their equipment was not in much better shape: Hoses had burst, carts had burned, and two of the steam engines were too damaged to use.

That morning, even before the fire was completely out, the *Chicago Tribune* ran its Sunday paper with special coverage of the event, which they prematurely dubbed the "Great Fire." The first paragraph proved eerily prophetic:

> For days past alarm has followed alarm, but the comparatively trifling losses have familiarized us to the pealing of the Courthouse bell, and we had forgotten that the absence of rain for three weeks had left everything in so dry and inflammable a condition that a spark might set a fire which would sweep from end to end of the city.

Like the thousands of depleted spectators trudging home from the fire, and the displaced homeowners seeking new shelter, and the firefighters dropping into a deep but too-brief sleep, the *Tribune* reporters knew that a worse disaster was possible. But even they could not have guessed that this editorial would be the last they would ever print in their "fireproof" offices.

THE FIRE CHIEF

Robert A. Williams was the chief fire marshal at this fateful time in the city's history. Williams was a tall, strongly built Canadian with kind brown eyes and a beard and moustache. He had been fighting fires in Chicago for about 20 years and had worked his way up to the department's top position. He had no delusions about the seriousness of the situation. He understood that the force under his command—16 horse-drawn steamers, 6 hose carts, 4 hook-and-ladder companies, and 193 firefighters—was not big enough to cover 36 square miles of city. He knew the department needed more muscle, and he had asked the city for it. Specifically, he wanted more

Considered to be "fireproof," the Post Office and Custom House (*above*) was home to two federal offices and was destroyed by the fire. Salvaged walls were later used to build a local theater in the city.

fire hydrants, more firemen, and a building inspection bureau that would force builders to quit building with wood. He also wanted fireboats that could patrol the river and shoot streams of water into the air. Unfortunately, the city council was more interested in fueling the growth of the city than in ensuring its safety, and they refused every one of Williams's requests. (Later, an inquiry revealed that Williams's fireboats could have prevented the fire from crossing the river, holding the damage to about 20 city blocks instead of 1,687 acres.)

This left the fire chief with only one strategy for beating the hundreds of fires that broke out each year. That was to get to fires quickly, before they could overwhelm his little brigade of horse carts and hoses. Or, as Williams himself put it, "[Strike] it before it gets the start of you. That is the only secret in putting out fires." He clearly took his own advice to heart. As Chicago historian Robert Cromie explains in his classic account of the Great Fire, Williams did not get a lot of sleep. Whenever a night alarm sounded, he leaped from bed and put on his uniform, which included a long rubber coat with brass buttons, a pointy helmet that said "Chief Fire Marshal," and a brass speaking horn that he used as an amplifier. He was out the door in two or three minutes flat, and he often went out several times the same night.

Since speed was the only strategy for beating fires, everything depended on the city's alarm system. In 1871, the city had a nerve network of 172 fire-alarm boxes that were mounted at stores and other businesses throughout the city. If a fire broke out, someone had to run to the nearest one of these entrusted businesses and convince the owner to unlock the box and pull the hook. This sent an electrical signal to the courthouse downtown, where an operator was always on duty. Upon getting the alarm, the operator sent a signal to the engine companies, then tolled the 11,000-pound courthouse bell—once for a small fire, twice for a larger one, and three times for a fire that was out of control. As a more old-fashioned backup system, the fire companies posted watchmen on their roofs, and the city kept watchmen on the courthouse roof at all times, peering out into the night for the telltale signs of light and smoke.

On October 8, 1871, the Sunday afternoon following the Lull and Holmes fire, Fire Chief Williams went home and tried to sleep. But in his usual, dedicated way, he woke up several times and attended to the business of the fire department. After helping to put a small fire out in the South Side of the city, he climbed onto a wagon and headed home again. The wind began to rise, and he tugged his helmet down to keep it from blowing away. Then, as Robert Cromie reports, he turned to his driver and said, "We are going to have a burn. I can feel it in my bones." Back at his house, he confessed the same fear to his wife: "I am going to bed early," he said. "I feel as though I have got to be out between this and morning, the way the wind is blowing." Then he laid out his uniform, so he would be able to put it back on in a hurry.

THE COW BARN

Around 9:00 P.M., while the fire chief was sleeping, Daniel "Peg Leg" Sullivan sat down on a wooden sidewalk, pausing a few moments to enjoy the strangely hot night and its humming wind. Daniel was a 26-year-old drayman, or cart driver, who had lost his leg in a railroad accident. As he sat down on the wooden boards, he adjusted his peg leg to make himself comfortable and leaned back against a fence that ran behind the sidewalk. Before him, the West Side neighborhood of poor Irish immigrants was going to sleep, the lamps blinking out one by one. Daniel yawned: He, too, would have to go to bed in a few minutes, so he could get up early, hitch up his horses, and drive his cart for the oil company.

Across the street from Daniel were two houses—one facing the street and another tucked behind it. The one facing the street was the McLaughlins' house, and fiddle music was floating from the windows. The McLaughlins were having a little party to celebrate the arrival of a relative from Ireland. The house behind that was the O'Leary house, where Catherine and Patrick O'Leary lived with their five children. All their lights were already out. And just beyond that was the O'Learys' barn, where Catherine O'Leary kept her five milk cows and her horse and calf. Daniel knew that barn very well. His mother kept a cow in there, and some nights Daniel would stop in and feed it hay.

Now, as Daniel slumped against the fence, feeling increasingly sleepy, he thought he saw something strange. It looked like a yellow tongue of light, waving from the side of the O'Leary barn. Watching it, his body began to grow stiff with worry, and he straightened up off the fence, straining for a better look. The yellow light flickered and wagged in the darkness—it was a flame, no doubt about it. His heart started to pound as he scrambled from the wooden sidewalk into the street. He struggled to make his wooden leg move faster. "FIRE! FIRE! FIRE!" he shouted into the wind.

Daniel cut across the darkened lawn of the O'Leary property, making his way straight for the barn. As he stepped inside he felt a blast of heat and saw a tempest of flames whipping back and forth in the hayloft. Only hours earlier, a deliveryman had brought three tons of timothy hay to the O'Leary barn, and now it was burning in a crackling flash. It was too late to save the barn, but Daniel thought he might be able to save some of the terrified animals. There were four cows to his left, and he managed to untie two of them before the heat became too intense. He yelled at the cows, but they stood frozen, refusing to flee the barn. The flames were too strong now—if he did not leave the barn immediately, Daniel knew he would die with the petrified animals. He ran for the alleyway door, but his peg leg slipped and sent him sprawling. He coughed in the thick black smoke and tried to stand. Before

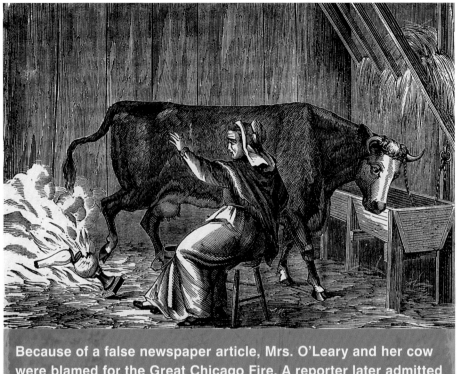

Because of a false newspaper article, Mrs. O'Leary and her cow were blamed for the Great Chicago Fire. A reporter later admitted to printing the incorrect information. Although several neighbors were also suspected of starting the blaze, and Mrs. O'Leary was exonerated, she is still commonly blamed for the disaster.

he get could get his balance, a calf came running from behind and banged his hip. The animal's back was on fire and it was howling in pain and fear. Daniel grabbed the rope around its neck and pulled it with him toward the barn door. Together they burst into the alley, where Daniel slapped the flames out on the calf's back.

At last the neighbors began to emerge from their houses, and one of them, a man named Dennis Regan, ran into the O'Learys' house and woke the family. Mr. O'Leary came out into the yard and scratched his head in disbelief. "Kate!" he yelled. "The barn is afire." Mrs. O'Leary and her children ran from the house. The neighbors helped Mr. O'Leary throw buckets of water onto his house, which had already begun to smolder. Mrs. O'Leary, faced with the loss of her barn and livestock, tried at least to save a new wagon that was parked behind the barn, but the searing heat would not let her near enough. Soon the sparks flew and started the wagon, a shed, and another barn on fire. Then the flames sped along the wooden fence to the Daltons' house, the first actual house to catch fire, and the Great Chicago Fire had begun.

To this day, no one knows what started the fire in Mrs. O'Leary's barn, though there are countless theories. Historians and amateur sleuths have guessed that a spark flew from a nearby chimney, or that the new timothy hay spontaneously combusted, or even that a comet hit the barn. Other theories

Mrs. O'Leary in Song

Neighborhood children may have first invented and spread the story about Mrs. O'Leary and the cow kicking over the lamp, according to historian John J. McKenna. Whether or not this is true, children have always relished the tale. In the decades after the fire, they could often be heard reciting these verses, which were part of a Great Chicago Fire version of "This Is the House That Jack Built":

This is the hovel dingy and dreary,
That sheltered the famous Mrs. O'Leary,
That milked the cow forlorn and weary,
That kicked the lamp, that started the
Fire, that burned the city.

involve intruders who supposedly snuck into the barn for different reasons—to gamble, to steal milk for oyster stew, or to let their new terrier kill the rats—and then dropped a match or lamp. The *Chicago Times* published an article claiming that the fire was a communist plot, secretly started by an organization called the Société Internationale. But the earliest rumor, and the one that stuck, was that Mrs. O'Leary was milking a cow that kicked over a lamp, which spilled its burning kerosene over the hay. Never mind that Mrs. O'Leary was asleep at the time the fire started. And never mind that Mrs. O'Leary was found completely innocent by an inquiry conducted in the months after the fire. The truth was the city seemed eager to pin the blame on someone, and a poor Irish immigrant was a good enough scapegoat. The newspapers had a great time with the story, inventing more and more details, describing Mrs. O'Leary as an "old hag" and her husband as "a stupid-looking sort of a man."

But as unfair as this treatment was, there was no stopping the rumor about the cow in the barn, which spread as quickly and decisively as the fire itself. As the *Chicago Journal* put it: "Even if it were an absurd rumor, forty miles wide of the truth, it would be useless to attempt to alter the verdict of history. Fame has seized [Mrs. O'Leary] and appropriated her, name, barn, cow, and all." Even today, more than a century later, if you ask anyone about the Great Chicago Fire, they will probably tell you it all began when Mrs. O'Leary's cow kicked over a lamp.

3

"Everything Went Wrong!"

Two doors down from the O'Learys', William Lee was closing the window blinds in his child's bedroom when he saw flames shooting from the roof of the O'Learys' barn. Lee called to his wife to watch the infant and bolted from the house. He sprinted past the thickly clustered cottages, pigsties, and corncribs, his feet pounding on the wooden boards, his heart thumping in his chest. Although the fire had already been burning for 10 minutes, Lee was the first one to think of calling in an alarm.

DEADLY MISTAKES

William Lee was breathless when he got to Goll's Pharmacy, but he managed to ask Bruno Goll, the pharmacist, for the key to the alarm box. Goll refused, saying that a fire engine had already driven past. This angered Lee. After all, what good was the city's new alarm system if no one pulled the lever? But he had no time to argue with Goll. He had to look after his own family. He ran home and moved his wife and 17-month-old child out of the house to a vacant lot away from the fire. Mrs. Lee brought a cradle for the child, and as she rocked it in the vacant lot, a singed calf sidled up and nuzzled her. It was the poor animal Sullivan had rescued from the barn, homesick and lonely without its parents, and it would stay with the family all night.

Bruno Goll later told the Fire Commission that he turned in an alarm after Lee left. But if this was true, the signal never reached the courthouse. In fact, no alarm reached the courthouse from the city's alarm boxes until 40 minutes into the fire, when the flames were nearly out of control.

Meanwhile, at the lookout on the courthouse roof, Mathias Schafer, the 40-year-old watchman, was conversing with two of his friends. One of them pointed to an orange glow far away in the West Side and said it looked like a fire. But Schafer assured his friend not to worry. It was only the glow of the gasworks, he said, reflected off the clouds. Changing the topic, he offered his visitors a tour of the roof, and the group strolled around the giant, four-faced clock.

Down on the first floor, the young fire-alarm operator also had visitors. His name was William Brown, and he was playing guitar for his 16-year-old sister Sarah and her friend Martha. Humming along with the music, Sarah glided over to the window, where she happened to notice a pulsing orange light across town. She asked her brother if it was a fire, but Brown, like his partner on the roof, assured her it was nothing to worry about. It was only the embers from last night's fire, he said.

When Schafer came back to his starting point on the tower, red flames were already leaping in the west. He grabbed his spyglass in a panic, quickly trying to pinpoint the fire's location. But it was a dark, moonless night, the flames were far away, and the pile of embers from the previous night's blaze was blocking his view. After studying the situation a few moments, he made the best guess he could, calling down the speaking tube to Brown and telling him to strike Box 342. Unfortunately, this was a mile away from the fire's actual location. While Brown struck the alarm, Schafer continued to

William Lee, a neighbor of Mrs. O'Leary's, saw the fire from his home and immediately ran to Bruno Goll's drugstore *(above)* to use the fire alarm in the building to alert authorities. Lee later claimed that the owner prevented him from using the alarm, since another location with an alarm was closer. The wasted time led to the quick spread of the fire.

study the flames, uneasy with his choice. A few minutes later, he called down again, ordering Brown to strike Box 319. This was still not the exact location, but it was close enough that it might have saved Chicago, had Brown simply done as he was told. But Brown decided the extra alarm would confuse everyone, and he stubbornly refused to strike it. This foolish mistake sealed the fate of the city. Powerful steam engines that might have dowsed the fire in its infancy instead sped off in the wrong direction or else waited in their stations, believing the fire was in some other district.

"HANG ON TO HER BOYS!"

At least one good thing came of striking Box 342: It sent a signal to Chief Williams's private fire alarm in his bedroom. When the gong sounded, Williams's wife elbowed him in the ribs. "Robert, FIRE!" she cried. Williams must have been tired of hearing this word, but he jumped out of bed with his usual speed, and moments later, he was standing outside waiting for his crew.

When Williams's wagon arrived at the fire, after first heading in the wrong direction due to the erroneous signal, three steam engines—the *Little Giant*, the *Chicago*, and the *Economy*—were already on the scene and spraying water, along with a hose cart called the *America*. Luckily, all these crews had ignored the alarm and simply followed the flames. Williams ran among the crews to provide desperately needed leadership. He shouted encouraging words to the *Chicago* crew, then ran to the pipemen of the *America*. "Hang on to her boys! She is gaining on us!" At that moment, the *Illinois* steamer arrived, and Williams ordered its crew to take a fireplug at Des Plaines and Taylor, and aim its hoses at a half-incinerated building. "Hang on to her here!" he yelled.

But the heat was growing insufferable. The jets of water seared into steam before they even reached the buildings. And the fire had sucked all the oxygen out of the air, making the firemen fight for each lung-scorching breath. "Marshal, I don't believe we can stand it here!" one of the pipe men gasped.

"Stand it as long as you can!" said Williams.

The yellow tongues of flame were hungrily lapping up a dozen homes, barns, and sheds, with plumes of black smoke coursing from their roofs. Two firefighters placed a door between themselves and the flames like a mighty shield. This worked well for a minute or two, until the door exploded into flames, singeing their hands and forcing them to drop the door and retreat. Their clothes were smoldering, and one of the men reached up to find his leather hat twisted out of shape by the blast of heat. Just then the horses reared in a panic, the hair singed from their bodies.

Fire Chief Williams had only been there a few minutes, but he could tell this was no longer a one-alarm fire. "Turn in a second alarm!" he yelled. "This is going to spread!"

The foreman of the *America* dropped what he was doing and ran to Bruno Goll's drugstore. But on that fateful night, confusion seemed to hover over the alarm boxes. Instead of sending the secret two-alarm fire signal, the foreman sent another one-alarm signal! Meanwhile, down at the courthouse, young William Brown was growing concerned about the spreading ocean of light. He decided to strike the two-alarm signal on his own, but stubbornly stuck with his original mistake. He struck box 342.

The fire surged from DeKoven Street to the south side of Taylor Street. The homes on the north side of Taylor were already starting to smolder, a warning sign that they would soon burst into flames. The fire marshal knew that if the fire crossed Taylor Street it would quickly double in size.

He called out to Charley Anderson, the fireman whose hat had just twisted in the heat. "Charley, come out as fast as possible. Wet the other side of the street or it will burn!"

Charley raced into the street, but before he could wet the houses, his hose sputtered, dribbled, and stopped altogether.

Unknown to Charley, the steam engine *Waubansia* had just arrived and taken over the fire plug that Charley's hose cart was using. This was common practice, since the fireplugs needed to go to the powerful steam engines, rather than the little hose carts, but the timing could not have been worse.

As if this were not bad enough, at the same instant, the water of the *Chicago* steamer began to slow to a trickle. In this case, a broken pump appeared to be at fault. The foreman of the *Chicago* ordered the engineer to hit the balky pump with a

The Great Chicago Fire sparked national trends in fire safety and improvements in municipal fire departments and their equipment. One of the many factors that led to the devastation in 1871 involved an overworked and understaffed fire brigade with insufficient equipment to fight a fire of such magnitude.

hammer. The engineer swung the hammer with all his might. For a moment, the two men held their breath in expectation, and then, miraculously, the pump began to chug again.

But it was too late. The momentary absence of water from the *America* and *Waubansia* had given the fire the advantage it was looking for, and all at once, five houses on the north side of the street burst into flames, yielding to the heat like popcorn kernels. The fire had crossed Taylor Street.

Soon there were new problems. Some of the worn-out hoses burst, and the firemen had to tie blankets around the holes. More and more steam was necessary to maintain the pressure in these leaky hoses. Spectators helped by chopping up sidewalks and fences to fuel the great steam engines, but the firemen were losing ground.

Williams tried to keep a cool head. He still had only five steamers, three hose carts, and a hook-and-ladder company. Like a chess player with an insufficient number of pieces, he had to consider his options carefully. He decided to place his five steamers at the corners of the fire: the *Economy* steamer at the southeast corner, the *Little Giant* at the southwest, the *Chicago* and *Illinois* at the northwest, and the *Waubansia* at the northeast. In this way, he hoped to create a belt of water surrounding the blaze and flood it with everything he had.

FIRE DEVILS!

Now that all of Taylor Street was on fire, the heat was increasing, and it caused the updrafting wind to surge. Despite the drought, the wooden buildings, the exhausted firemen, and a series of errors at the alarm boxes and lookouts that might have made the Marx Brothers blush, it was the wind that played the starring role in this terrible night. The bone-dry wind had been picking up speed all day. It was blowing north-northeast. If you drew a line from the O'Leary barn to the heart of the city, that was the precise direction the wind was blowing, as if it were determined to rake the flames over every building in the city. And what a wind it was! Witnesses described twisting gusts that ripped the roofs off buildings and threw burning mattresses and furniture hundreds of feet into the air. The actual wind never got faster than 30 miles an hour that night, but the witnesses were not lying. What they were actually describing were convection whirls, or "fire devils"—superheated columns of air that rise with a twisting, tornado-like motion. Fire devils formed due to the extraordinary heat of the fire, which reached 2,500°F in some places—hot enough to melt marble and steel, or to make trees explode from the heat of their resin. When masses of air are heated to such high temperatures, especially when they are trapped between the shear faces of buildings, they rise in twisting columns, sucking the cooler air in at their bases. And these gusting columns do indeed behave like tornadoes or hurricanes.

It was the fire devils that ripped the roofs and cornices off buildings and created solid walls of fire 100 feet high. As the fire crossed Taylor Street, small fire devils were already beginning to form. Chunks of burning material, called firebrands, began to fly off the buildings and twirl overhead, showering down like red rain. As Williams and company fought the blaze on one street, the red rain streamed over their heads and moved the fire to a street farther north. The firebrands helped spread the fire from Taylor Street to Forquer Street, to Ewing Street, to Polk Street, and on and on. Each time the firemen thought they might get the flames under control, the firebrands leapfrogged over their heads. When the fire had traveled six blocks, Williams and his team raced north to meet it at Harrison Street, where he ran into Commissioner James Chadwick.

"Don't you know the fire is getting ahead of you?" asked Chadwick.

"Yes," Williams confessed. "It is getting ahead of me in spite of all I can do. It is just driving me along."

At about 10:00 P.M., a two-foot-long piece of wood flew four blocks over the firemen's heads and landed on the steeple of St. Paul's Catholic Church. The steeple rose high over the city—if it burned, it would transmit firebrands far and wide. Fire Chief Williams ordered a hook-and-ladder truck to hurry to the church. Once the ladder was in place, firefighters scrambled up with hoses and quickly extinguished the fire, then put it out a second time when the flames reappeared minutes later. When they were finished, they began to lower their ladder,

"An Iron Man Couldn't Have Stood It."

After the fire, many of the newspapers and early histories accused the firefighters of being drunk during the fire. The story went that, after the Lull and Holmes fire, the firemen had celebrated by going out to drink whiskey instead of going home to bed. But when Fire Marshal Williams was asked about this alleged intoxication in an interview, he offered a spirited defense that is probably closer to the truth: "But bless your soul . . . the heat was awful; 'twas like hell, and the firemen's eyes were red with the dust and fire, so that many of them were most blind. The hair was scorched off their faces, and they stuck to their machines like bull dogs, and worked them till they couldn't stand it any longer. Yes, sir, and they did stagger, for they were clean beat, and many of them had to go home for the exhaustion from the heat. They were tired, too, from the fire of the night before, and then to give the same men such a long pull again, why, an iron man couldn't have stood it."

but in another striking piece of bad luck, the ladder fell and broke into pieces. As one of the firemen later put it, "From the very beginning of that fatal fire, everything went wrong!" The firemen watched the steeple nervously, and sure enough, about three minutes later, flames popped up again. Without a ladder, there was little they could do. They tried to throw a stream from the street, but the wind was too strong, and the water would not reach the flames. There was nothing to do but watch the roof catch fire and carry the statues of saints and other relics out of the church and into the street.

As the wooden saints were being deposited among the crowd, an elderly Irish woman asked what was burning. Someone told her it was St. Paul's.

"Oh," she said, smiling, "God will put it out."

Minutes later, the roof caved in.

"NOTHING CAN STOP IT NOW."

The streets were quickly filling not only with spectators and wooden saints but also with furniture and housewares. It was customary practice among Chicagoans to carry everything out of their houses into the center of the streets during a fire. The idea was that, if the house were destroyed, at least the family would still have its possessions. The result of this strange practice was a thick backbone of blankets, mattresses, chairs, and crates running up the center of each wooden street, inviting the flames to hurry along, while impeding the firemen. The wind casually plucked items from this gigantic, flaming yard sale and hurled them against buildings, instantly igniting them.

The streets were also filling with refugees who had lost their homes. One reporter, Joseph Chamberlin, described the scene on Ewing Street: "Female inhabitants were rushing out almost naked, imploring spectators to help them on with their burdens of bed quilts, cane-bottomed chairs, iron kettles, etc. Drays were thundering along in the single procession which the narrowness of the street allowed, and all was confusion."

While the fire may have started in a section on the West Side, the shifting winds and fiery debris lit up the South and North Sides. This left a section of the West Side safe, but inaccessible to those who needed to escape the fire. A depiction of the view of the fire from the West Side of Chicago *(above)* shows the chaos and confusion people experienced as the fire grew in different parts of the city.

In a vacant square a little farther on, Chamberlin encountered a different brand of chaos:

> The fire had reached a better section, and many people of the better class were among those who had gathered a few of their household goods on that open square. Half a dozen rescued pianos were watched by delicate ladies, while the crowd still surged in every direction. Two boys, themselves intoxicated, reeled about, each bearing a small cask of

whisky out of which he insisted upon treating everybody he met. Soon more casks of whisky appeared, and scores of excited men drank deeply of their contents. The result was, of course, that an equal number of drunken men were soon impeding the flight of the fugitives.

There was a party atmosphere across the river as well, where the denizens of the South Side slums had come to watch the spectacle. The crowds on the riverbank grew so rowdy that, at one point, the firemen had to turn their hoses on them. Although 20 city blocks were aflame, the South Side partyers felt safe because the fire was on the other side of the river, and there was no way for it to cross. Besides, everyone thought the fire would end when it reached the burned-out area from last night's fire, where it would run out of fuel.

As St. Paul's burned, firebrands took to the wind. Like a swarm of locusts, they descended on two furniture factories,

Chicago's Divides

The Chicago River splits the city into three main sections. The O'Leary family lived in the West Side, which was crowded full of working-class neighborhoods. The South Side contained the city's worst slums and also the main business district with its theaters, shops, and hotels. And the North Side contained a large immigrant community, along with the stately mansions and beautiful gardens of the wealthy. Together, the three districts made up downtown Chicago, where about one-third of all Chicagoans lived and where the Great Fire ran its terrible course.

which in turn fired the Bateham Mills. The mills were huge—one and a half acres of kindling, furniture boards, and shingles, piled 25 feet high like ready-made bonfires. Nearby, crowded along the riverbanks, were more lumberyards, paint shops, wagon shops, saloons, and furniture factories—even a match factory. Fire Chief Williams positioned steamers outside the mills, then went inside to assess the situation: "I went in there, but the fire was coming down thicker than any snowstorm you ever saw, and the yard between the two mills was all filled with shavings, and chunks of fire came in of all sizes, from the length of your arm down to three inches."

In the end, there was not much Williams could do to save Bateham Mills. Increasingly, there was nothing he could do about any of this. When one of his firemen asked what to do about the hose they'd lost, he answered sadly, "God only knows." Mr. Bateham, the owner of the mills, also seemed resigned. As he watched the flaming scraps of his empire stream over the river, he turned and shook his head. "The materials from this mill will fire the South Side," he said. "Nothing can stop it now."

4. South Side Inferno

Mr. Bateham's prediction soon came true. The wind lifted detritus, or debris, from the burning mills, carried it high over the river, and dropped it on the South Side. One chunk landed on a three-story horse stable, quickly turning it to a shimmering pool of embers. Another burning shingle landed on the gasworks, which would have exploded if the superintendent had not heroically entered the building and transferred the gas to a different part of town.

Other windborne sparks fell like hail on Conley's Patch, the city's most infamous vice district. This wooden maze of shanties was filled with brothels, pawnshops, gambling dens, and saloons. It was a place where Chicago went to sin, and the flames thrashed it like the very wrath of God. In his book *City of the Century*, Donald Miller describes the scene vividly:

As the wind-driven fire raced through this dismal slum, women and children rushed out into the streets screaming in terror and clutching rosaries, crucifixes, and what simple possessions they had managed to get their hands on—a Sunday dress, a child's rag doll, a clutch of family

49

letters. Most of them escaped, but a few—mostly the sick and the elderly—were overrun by a moving wall of fire one thousand feet wide and over a hundred feet high. It was in Conley's Patch that the "death harvest" began.

Before long, the streets were a fiery chaos. People pushed past each other, trying desperately to flee. The air was so hot

Not a Single Photograph

One of the mysteries about the Great Fire is the fact that there is not a single photograph of the event. There are innumerable drawings of the fire, and plenty of photos of Chicago before and after, but the flames and the chaos were never captured on film. In their book *The Great Fire*, Herman Kogan and Robert Cromie suggest several possible explanations. The cameras of the day may not have been able to operate in such intense heat. Or photographers may have been too frightened to stop and set them up. After all, in 1871 the cameras were not small and portable like those today—they were large, clumsy cabinets with legs. But the most likely explanation is that even successful photographers probably had to drop their cameras and run for their lives during the evacuation. If so, it is interesting to note that one visual artist, John R. Chapin, had cooler nerves than the photographers, since he sat beside the Randolph Street Bridge and calmly drew one of the most famous images of the fire. With a steady pencil, he depicted a mass of people and animals surging over the bridge, while flames erupted from the buildings all around him.

In this famous illustration, the people of Chicago flood Randolph Street Bridge in a bid to save themselves and whatever they could carry in their arms. A reporter for the *Chicago Evening Post*, Joseph Edgar Chamberlin, described the scene by saying, "A torrent of humanity was pouring over the bridge." Many of Chicago's citizens headed out toward the east, in order to reach Lake Michigan, while others settled outside the city in western prairies.

they had to cover their mouths to breathe, and the falling embers caught their clothes on fire. Flames shot up between the sidewalk boards and devoured the piles of furniture. Lost children wandered aimlessly, crying for their parents. People kicked at the fat brown rats that were pouring from the buildings. Others struggled to pile their belongings into horse-drawn wagons, which jockeyed for position and crashed into each other on the avenues.

The great inferno seemed to be coming from every direction at once. "You couldn't see anything over you but fire," one of the firemen later said. "No clouds, no stars, nothing but fire." Witnesses described jets of flame that shot the length of a city block before striking a building and encasing it, or massive sheets of red that fell over entire streets, incinerating 40 or 50 homes in just a few minutes. Everyone remembered the strength of the fire devils, which pinned one little girl to a girder on a bridge and threw a man against a lamppost with such force that both man and lamppost collapsed in the street.

In the midst of all the twisting, racing flames, people were uncertain which way to run. To add to the confusion, several of the bridges and tunnels had already burned and become impassible. Meanwhile, up and down the river, tugboats were helping to pull the ships in a long procession to the lake. Many of the masts and riggings were already on fire, and sailors were leaping into the river to save themselves. The operators of the rotating bridges had to choose between letting the ships pass or letting the people cross. Each time they turned the bridges to let the ships through, cries went up from the desperate masses waiting on the riverbanks. In some places, the river itself was burning. It had become so polluted with oil and industrial chemicals, the very water was flammable.

THE COURTHOUSE

As it engulfed the gasworks and Conley's Patch, the fire grew bigger, hotter, and faster, and continued its advance north and east toward the magnificent downtown district. This region contained the great hotels, including the nine-story Palmer House, seven-story Sherman House, and the very unlucky Tremont House, which had already burned to the ground and been rebuilt twice before. These buildings may not seem tall by today's standards, but the skyscraper had not been invented yet, and at the time, they were considered engineering marvels. In fact, with the exception of New York City, the downtown district had no rival in America. On State Street, which had been created in imitation of Parisian boulevards, dozens of stores and businesses offered exotic imports for the wealthy. Everything from Chinese silks to Belgian glass could be found in the walnut cases of stores such as Field and Leiter's, where boys in blue uniforms with brass buttons stood at attention, waiting to whisk the doors open. The downtown was also home to most of the city's theaters, banks, government buildings, and newspapers. Strangely enough, a number of these buildings had been proudly declared fireproof, since they had been built with iron girders and other flame-resistant features.

Chief among the "fireproof" buildings was the courthouse itself, a marble behemoth rising like a castle in the center of the city. With its domed clock tower and five-ton bell, the courthouse was the city's grandest showpiece. It housed not only the fire-alarm lookout but also most of the city offices and, in the basement, the county jail.

William Brown, the fire-alarm operator, had already left the building, but not before finally tolling a three-alarm warning. Once again he tolled for Box 342, though it hardly mattered now. The sky was bright as day, and no one needed a bell to tell them their city was being devoured.

As for Schafer, the night watchman, he and several other men valiantly remained on the courthouse roof, trying to douse the bright orange cinders using only buckets and brooms. On all the neighboring rooftops, men could be seen doing the same, dipping their brooms into buckets of water and swiping at the embers like a frantic team of chimney sweeps. The men worked feverishly, pausing only to slap out the flames on their clothing. When at last a firebrand blew into a broken window in the clock tower, it ignited a blaze that poured across the courthouse roof like water. Schafer and the others barely escaped. Finding the stairs already on fire, they slid down the banister, burning their hands and faces. Schafer raced into the operations room, where flames were already popping through cracks in the ceiling, and set the courthouse bell to automatic,

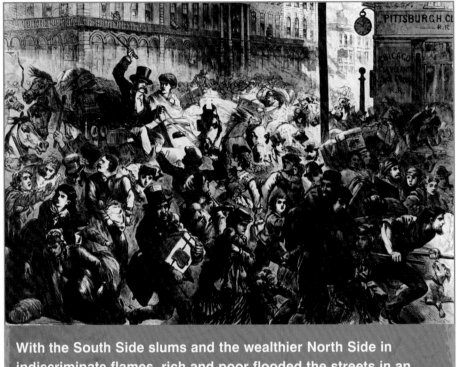

With the South Side slums and the wealthier North Side in indiscriminate flames, rich and poor flooded the streets in an attempt to reach Lake Michigan or any other safe area. Above, people from all classes take to the streets around the luxurious Sherman House hotel.

making it ring over and over. He then left the doomed building and lent a hand to Fire Marshal Williams, who at that moment was trying to save the Sherman House hotel.

In the courthouse basement, smoke began to pour into the jail. The prisoners banged on the bars, screaming and begging for their freedom. Hearing their cries, people on the street picked up a plank and used it like a battering ram to try and break down the jailhouse door. The jail keeper refused to unlock the cells, until finally the mayor sent orders that all the prisoners were to be released into the streets, except for the murderers, who were led in chains to the North Side. The non-murderers could hardly believe their luck. "One of the liberated men fainted from relief," while "others were stunned by their freedom and moved as if in a daze," writes Robert Cromie in his book *The Great Chicago Fire*.

At the same time the prisoners were being given their freedom, the owner and staff of a burning jewelry store were loading wagons with all of their store's jewels. But the firemen would not let them drive off because the street was filled with canvas water hoses that the heavy wagons might damage. Faced with no choice but to abandon his inventory, the store owner told the fleeing prisoners to help themselves to the precious mounds of diamonds, pearls, and gold. "The prisoners must have thought they had reached Paradise," writes Cromie. "Tossed out of jail and plied with jewels."

The Melted Bell

After its earsplitting crash from the tower, the half-melted courthouse bell was recovered and sold to H.S. Everhart & Company. The company melted the bell down to make tiny working models of the original, each smaller than a penny, and sold them as souvenirs. Other mementos, such as rings and tiny fire hats, were also made from the bell. In fact, so many "melted-bell" souvenirs flooded the market, people began to grow skeptical of their authenticity. The *Chicago Times* commented wryly, "It is safe to say that enough pieces of the courthouse bell have been distributed throughout the world to make up a whole chime that should outring the Bow Bells of London."

As the accessorized criminals slipped away to start new lives, the limestone walls of their courthouse prison dripped and melted into the streets. At 2:12 A.M., the hands slid off one of the clock faces. Several minutes later, the great iron bell crashed down through the tower, landing in the vacated basement prison with a thundering crash that could be heard a mile away and sending up a volcano blast of flame.

"THERE GO THE BELLS AGAIN"

The fire department was overwhelmed. Having moved their equipment over the river, they did not know where to focus their efforts. It seemed that everything, everywhere was on fire simultaneously. The wind blocked them from walking up some of the streets, and it stopped the streams from their hoses, throwing the water back in their faces. No longer able to sustain a carefully orchestrated defense, they broke into smaller, confused groups and tried to save individual buildings throughout the city. Fire Chief Williams and dozens of volunteers were working on the Sherman House, which was smoking but not yet burning, its white walls glowing a brilliant rose color as they mirrored the flames from the street.

Inside the hotel, many of the guests were only just stirring, having ignored the earlier alarms. "There go the bells again," one of the guests had earlier joked in the lobby.

Luckily a very calm and collected night clerk took charge. First, he put the hotel's most important papers in the vault. Then he went from room to room, waking each of the 300 guests. Five of the guests were sick elderly women who were confined to their beds, and the night clerk gave instructions for these defenseless individuals to be placed in a carriage and driven to safety. But when the carriage was gone, he had a sudden, powerful sense of unease. He chased after the driver and discovered there were four women, not five, in the carriage. He looked back at the hotel, where he knew the other woman must be trapped in her room. Long, orange flames were already snapping from the upper windows like dragon tongues. He grabbed a fire ax from one of the firemen and, with his assistant in tow, raced back to the hotel. The two men sprinted through the smoke-filled hallways and shattered the old woman's door with two hard swings of the ax. The poor invalid sat up in bed, terrified: She had not even realized there was a fire. Grabbing the pitcher and basin, they soaked her dress with water. Then they soaked the bed quilt, wrapped it around her, and carried her through the flaming corridors. She fainted as she was placed safely in the carriage, and the Sherman House collapsed moments later.

As went the Sherman House, so fell the other hotels. The marble stairways collapsed, the great glass domes imploded, and the steam-driven "vertical railways" (also known as elevators) locked up. Guests screamed and jumped over the banisters. Rich women emerged wearing all their wraps and jewels at once, their faces stained with smoke. At the Girard Hotel, a mother set her three children on a trunk in front of the building, telling them she was going back inside to get the last of their belongings, and not to leave till she came back. Sadly, she did not come back. As the fire drew closer, bystanders could not convince the children to abandon their post and finally had to carry them away, still crying for their mother.

One by one, the roofs of the banks, offices, and stores crashed down through the gutted shells of their buildings into the street. At the Western Union Office, a telegraph operator began the night's final message: "THE BLOCK IMMEDIATELY ACROSS THE STREET FROM THE TELEGRAPH OFFICE, ONE OF THE FINEST—" before running from the building. At the *Chicago Times*, the printers also wrote one final bulletin before going home to help their families: "THE VERY LATEST—The entire business portion of the city is burning up, and the TIMES building is doomed." The bulletin rolled off the presses, and less than an hour later, the building was reduced to a heap of charred timbers and powdered stone.

HALL OF FLAMES

Claire Innes was a clever and resourceful girl, but in all her 12 years she had never imagined anything like this. She and her parents and her little brothers and sister were running through the clamorous streets, each of them carrying a bundle of clothing wrapped in a tablecloth. They were trying to make it to the Clark Street Bridge and over the river to the North Side. Claire later wrote about the whole experience in a letter to her cousin, and historian Jim Murphy recounts the story, along with the key parts of the letter, in an adventure-packed book called *The Great Fire*. In her letter, Claire writes:

> We went two or three blocks, I don't remember how many . . . when movement became impossible. . . . Father told us to drop our bundles and hold hands, but I did not drop mine. The crowd moved forward a little, then people began turning and pushing against us. There was no resisting the crush and we were swept along. . . . I felt as a leaf in a great rushing river. . . . The wind was terrible, like a storm, and filled with cinders and fire. I held up my hands to keep them from my eyes. . . . [A] short, rough man grabbed at my bundle [but I] would not let it go. I called for Father and almost lost my bundle except that another man took hold of [the thief] and dragged him away. When I turned, I could not find Father or Mother or my sister or brothers. I ran down the sidewalk after them, calling their names and searching everywhere for a familiar face. They were gone—into the smoke and dark and falling fire.

The unthinkable had happened: Claire had been separated from her family. There was nothing to do but join the crowd in its crazy journey through the streets and alleyways. The crowd kept splitting into smaller and smaller groups as it advanced, each group choosing a different route which it considered safer. Claire ran first with one and then another, then finally got fed up and struck out on her own.

> I was all turned around and more tired than I can ever remember being. I was choking on the smoke and dust and I looked for a quiet place to rest. A little way along I came to a wide alley and went down it to an empty section filled with bricks and boards, barrels and ladders and such. . . . [A] man hurried past me without a word, followed by another. A third went by and said something to me over his shoulder, but I did not understand him as he spoke only German. When I looked back to where the men had just been, I saw smoke and fire blocking the entrance. I remember feeling very frightened by how quickly the fire had appeared, though this was nothing when compared to how I felt a moment later. I went to follow the men, but they were already gone and the other end of the alley was all fire and smoke, too.

Claire was trapped in a hall of fire. Both ends of the alley were sealed with flames, and the buildings on either side of her were already smoking. She knew she would have to think fast. It might be possible, she thought, to run through the blaze at one end of the alley, but when she tried, she found that "the heat was like that of an oven," and she had to stop. Then she pulled on the doorknob of one of the buildings, but it was bolted shut. Smoke was already pouring from the other doors, so she knew better than to try and open them. When the shower of embers grew thicker, she retreated to the only cover available, the pile of bricks in the middle of the alley: "I cannot say I actually decided to hide behind the bricks since I could not hear myself think in the terrible noise. I did not even look at the fire, but hid my face in the dirt and pulled my bundle, which I had retrieved, over my head. . . . [I] kept my head hidden beneath the bundle and said my prayers."

SYMPHONY OF TERROR

Claire Innes remained curled up in her cocoon of dirt and bricks, her head covered with the bundle of clothing. Although she could not see the flames directly, the flashing light must have made a ghastly shadow play under her makeshift blanket. But what was worse was the "terrible noise."

Believed to be fireproof, the courthouse *(above)* was destroyed by the fire. As the building began to burn and its bell fell from the tower, the watchman slid down staircase banisters to escape. The mayor had already ordered all criminals, except for the murderers, to be released from the prison in the basement.

The noise of the Great Fire is legendary. There was the pop and crackle of burning wood, and the roar of the flames themselves, which witnesses compared to waves crashing in a storm. Windows shattered, and oil barrels and liquor casks exploded through the night like gunfire. Then there was the sound of the great city itself, falling to the ground in pieces: the caving roofs, the rumbling-down walls, the apartment buildings that twisted in the heat, then heaved their upper floors away.

The cries of the animals were especially sad. Historian Robert Cromie describes the sudden burning of a pet store: "[The store] burned with all its inhabitants: parrots, macaws, mockingbirds, sparrows, canaries, several monkeys, and an assortment of choice poultry. It was said that as the fire approached, the trapped animals set up a hideous cry of anguish, just before a blast of superheated air struck the building and silenced them forever." The situation was not much better on the streets. Horses screamed in their burning stables or broke free and slammed through the crowd, kicking and biting. Dogs howled and cocks crowed, confused by the permanent sunrise. "Cats were seen leaping fences or racing across rooftops pursued by flames" writes Cromie, "but many chose to die rather than desert their homes." And then there were the human cries: people yelling for help, children crying for their parents, and everyone mourning their losses.

At least some of these sounds must have been part of the terrible noise that Claire Innes heard. But she did not uncover her head, and she did not come out until the alley had cooled off slightly. When she finally emerged, after perhaps an hour, the buildings were almost completely gutted. The greatest danger was past, but there were new challenges to face:

My legs and arms and back [were] all burnt where my dress caught fire. . . . I put out the fire and made ready to leave, which was not easy, as the [alleyway] openings were blocked with brick and burning wood and smoke. I called [for help] again and again and at last a voice called back to me through the smoke. He told me to stand away from there as a wall of the building might fall on me, and that was all. This made me even more alarmed, but I did not want to stay in the alley alone, so I began climbing. The bricks were still hot—very hot—but I found that if I did not stop [moving] my feet were not burnt so bad.

After scrambling over the heap of fiery bricks, Claire stood before the abandoned street. Many of the buildings were still burning, while others were reduced to a few craggy triangles, like the remaining pieces of a broken window. She took a deep breath. "Now," she said, "I had to find my family in all of this." She set off on a search through the burning city that would last two days but that would indeed end safely in the arms of her family.

5

"It Takes All Sorts"

Back in the courthouse block, the fire devils were lifting pieces of the burning buildings and carrying them north-northeast to the main trunk of the river. At 2:30 A.M., just as it had done at the southern arm of the river, the wind arched these flaming arrows over the water and onto the North Side. One landed in a railroad car filled with kerosene and another in a group of horse stables. The two fires shot up quickly, then flowed together and poured through the neighborhood. They were rushing straight toward the Waterworks, the source of all the city's water and the final link in its defense. It was as if the fire were "a wild beast intent on destroying its worst enemy, the enemy which it must either kill or be killed by," wrote historian Joseph Kirkland.

CHICAGO'S LAST HOPE

The Waterworks consisted of a great pump that pulled water through a tunnel under Lake Michigan, then pushed it to the top of a 130-foot water tower. The tower then fed all of the city's water mains using only the natural pressure of gravity. Both the tower and the pumping station were built of cream-colored stone and decorated with turrets and battlements like a fairy-tale castle. Like many of the great buildings down-town, the Waterworks was considered impervious to flame: It was built of stone, roofed with slate, and safely isolated by open areas on all sides. But like most of the city's "fireproof" buildings, it had a soft underbelly, a pine framework lying just beneath the armored exterior. When a flaming, 12-foot-long timber came sailing on the wind and crashed onto the roof, it was only a matter of minutes before it worked its way through to the timber frame beneath. A crew of men with water buckets labored briefly over this giant matchstick, then fled for their lives. There was no hope of saving the Waterworks once the timber was lit. And without water for the fire engines, there was no hope of saving the city.

When Fire Chief Williams got word that the Waterworks was burning, he did not want to believe it was true. He had to come over to the North Side and see for himself. His heart sank when he saw not only the Waterworks but also the surrounding neighborhood buried in flames. "Then I gave up all hopes of being able to save much of anything," he later testified. The once-mighty city was now completely at the mercy of the fire.

Many of the firefighters went home after they realized the water had stopped, but a few stayed on with Williams to continue the fight as best they could. By parking their steam engines beside the river and lake, they still managed, in some cases, to pump water up from these natural sources and save a number of buildings.

Another citizen took a different approach. James Hildreth, a Civil War veteran, decided the best way to stop the fire was to blow up the buildings in its path. This would starve the fire of fuel, creating a firebreak like those used to fight forest fires. In the early hours of the fire, he tagged along behind Williams, pestering him to authorize the scheme, until finally the exasperated fire chief told him, "Get your powder, then." Once he had permission, Hildreth ran off and got a wagon full of gunpowder kegs, which he carried into the basements of numerous buildings, laid a line of fuse, and started blowing things up with a force that shook the earth. At first he met with little success, managing only to blow the windows from a bank and a hole in the roof of a bakery. But he got better with practice, and soon he and his assistants were blowing up a building nearly every five minutes. Most of this destruction did little more than terrify everyone, but the leveling of homes at the southern edge of the fire probably helped stop its advance.

MADNESS AND POSSESSIONS

Throughout the night, as the South Side continued to burn, there were as many different actions as there were types of people. There were acts of heroism, like the barefoot girl who carried a box of puppies through the burning streets, or the many individuals who carried sick people through the fire in their arms. And there were acts of villainy, like the man who threw a glass of liquor on a girl whose hair had caught fire, making the alcohol flare up and cover her head with a blue flame. Many people seemed to go crazy with grief, like the woman who could not be prevented from running back into her burning home—three times she was removed, and three times she ran back, then did not come out again. Another woman was seen wandering the streets singing a nursery rhyme: "Chickery, Chickery, Crany Crow, I went to the well to wash my toe!" Others drowned their sorrows with alcohol, which was everywhere, since the saloon owners had wheeled their kegs into the streets to save them. One drunken man stood on a piano yelling about how the fire was "the friend of the poor man," until finally someone threw a bottle and knocked him off.

People also displayed very different reactions to losing everything they owned. After working all their adult lives to buy and furnish a home, they were left holding, in the case of

Built to provide the city with water from Lake Michigan, the Water Tower was another "fireproof" building that burned, but was not destroyed. As the only public building that withstood the fire in the burn zone, it became a symbol of survival in Chicago.

one woman, a bucket of lard and a deck of cards. James Washington Sheehan, a journalist at the time, describes the wide range of emotion he witnessed in the dispossessed:

> Some were philosophical, even merry, and witnessed the loss of their own property with a calm shrug of their shoulders, although the loss was to bring upon them irretrievable ruin. Others clenched their teeth together, and witnessed the sight with a sort of grim defiance. Others, who were strong men, stood in tears; and some became

fairly frenzied with excitement, and rushed about in an aimless manner, doing exactly what they would not have done in their cooler moments, and almost too delirious to save their lives from the general wreck.

As they abandoned their homes to the blaze, people had to choose a few favorite items to carry with them, and their choices were sometimes touching, sometimes practical, and sometimes simply odd. One man walked down the street with a rooster on his shoulder, and another with a window blind tucked under his arm. A preacher carried a sackful of his sermons, and a woman carried a frying pan and some muffin rings. One man wanted to save a chandelier, but his wife wisely suggested they carry a sewing machine instead. A particularly ambitious woman dressed in a white hat with pink roses, two silk dresses from Paris, and a mackintosh (raincoat) filled with silver spoons and opera glasses. Naturally, the wealth of items left behind—in the homes, in the businesses, and in all the luxurious stores—inevitably led to looting. It was simply too hard to resist all those unprotected treasures. Bystanders could walk into any department store and just help themselves. Or they could walk into the mansions of the wealthy and rifle through the closets and drawers. William Bross, one of the editors of the *Chicago Tribune*, discovered a thief coming through the front door of his house and looking suspiciously chubby. "My friend," he said, "you have on a considerable invoice of my clothes, with the hunting suit outside. Well, go along. You might as well have them as to let them burn."

But in the end, people who took things from the fire generally had to throw them back, since little could be carried through the storm of embers. Expensive luggage, books, furs, even money would catch fire and have to be dropped. As the flames hounded them up one avenue and down another, people shed the layers of jewels that were slowing them down or dropped the heavy trunks they were dragging. The streets filled with the discarded riches of a lifetime: all of it free for the taking, but none of it safe to take.

TO THE BRIDGES!

The only real hope of saving one's possessions was to get hold of a horse and wagon. Not surprisingly, the fight for these vehicles could be brutal. Desperate individuals threw each other from the wagons or forced the drivers to take them at gunpoint. At the same time, the drivers exploited the demand for their services. They would charge their passengers huge sums of money, then drive them only a few blocks, dump them and their belongings into the street, and speed away to pick up another helpless victim. They did not always get away with it. A young man named Thomas Foster wrote in a letter to his mother: "One expressman that we employed was going to drop our things out on the street after he got a few yards when one of my newly made acquaintances drew his revolver, and told him he would blow his brains out if he did. He drove quietly on after that." (This story is recounted in *The Great Chicago Fire and the Myth of Mrs. O'Leary's Cow* by Richard F. Bales.)

Alexander Frear also witnessed these "wagon wars" first-hand. When he and his nephew tried to climb into their wagon, they discovered that the horse was already unhitched and a stranger was sitting in the driver's seat. Frear grabbed hold of the horse's reigns just before the stranger could get away. The desperate man sprang from the wagon, punched Frear's nephew in the face, and ran off into the chaos of the streets. A little later, as the pair tried to drive through the South Side business district, people approached with their wallets out, imploring Frear to take carry some prized possession to safety. "Women came and threw packages into the vehicle," Frear recalls, "and one man with a boy hanging on to him caught our horse and tried to throw us out."

Moments later, a birdcage came flying from an upper window and hit Frear in the arm, causing the horse to spook and run headlong into another cart. There was a thundering crash as the two vehicles rammed together. Frear's nephew shot from the wagon into the street, and the terrified horse reared up and disappeared "with a leap like a panther."

Fortunately, Frear's nephew was only bruised, and the two were probably only too glad to continue their journey on foot. As they did so, Frear witnessed many painful sights. "I saw a woman kneeling in the street with a crucifix held up before her and the skirt of her dress burning while she prayed. We had barely passed before a runaway truck dashed her to the ground." When they ducked into the St. James Hotel, the lobby was filled with screaming women and children and with refugees who had fled from the burned-out neighborhoods. When the report came that the bridges were burning, cutting off all escape to the north and west, this news whipped the crowd into a frenzy. "Women, half-dressed, and many of them with screaming children, fled out of the building. There was a jam in the doorway, and they struck and clawed each other as if in self-defense." Frear was pushed out onto the street with the hysterical crowd and lost his nephew in the shuffle.

Frear moved on through streets that were "choked with people, yelling and moaning," and saw "huge flames pouring in from the side streets . . . with the force of a tremendous blowpipe." On one street, he saw a boy lying dead beneath a marble slab that had been thrown from an upper window. The boy wore white kid gloves, and gold cuff links spilled from his pockets. All around him, "the streets and sidewalks presented the most astonishing wreck. Valuable oil paintings, books, pet animals, musical instruments, toys, mirrors, and bedding were trampled under foot." Looking up, he saw several large department stores that ignited "suddenly all over . . . just as I have seen paper do that is held to the fire." Through the upper windows of one of these stores, a number of unsuspecting men could be seen unloading merchandise from the shelves just moments before the building was clothed in red.

As Alexander Frear finally approached a bridge to safety, morning had dawned over the burning city. The sunrise was doing nothing to quench the flames, however, and its tangerine light seemed insignificant in the hellish glare. Frear was swept along with the teeming masses onto the tar-soaked wooden surface. The bridge was already badly damaged. One railing was broken away, and as the crowd pressed forward, people were shoved over the side into the river. Down on the water, the boat captains mostly ignored this shower of pedestrians, "except to guard against anybody falling into their vessels."

Joseph Edgar Chamberlin described the same kind of pandemonium at the Randolph Street Bridge, where a "torrent of humanity" was trying to cross. Wagons were colliding "almost every moment," and women were struggling with heavy bundles on their backs. Each time the bridge rotated in the middle to let a ship pass through, a roar went up from the crowds on the bank, who were waiting anxiously to cross. But one of the strangest sights was an undertaker crossing with his stock of empty coffins. Unable to fit the black boxes into his cart, he

Adding Drama

Newspapers and magazines often sensationalized the events of the fire, creating fictional dramas to help sell copies. For example, the lurid cover illustration of one little booklet called "The Horrors of Chicago" depicted a woman clutching her baby and jumping to her death from a burning building, an arsonist setting new fires, and a dead man hung from a lamppost. Publications such as these helped fuel the notion that the fire had been one huge crime spree.

had hired a half-dozen boys to carry them, and as this crew crossed the bridge, the upright coffins could be seen "bobbing along just above the heads of the crowd." No one really needed such a stark reminder of the fact that death walked among them. "But," writes Chamberlin, "just as men in the midst of a devastating plague carouse over each new corpse, and drink to the next one who dies, so we laughed quite merrily at the ominous spectacle."

Both Frear and Chamberlin made it over their bridges, but not everyone was so lucky. In fact, 6 of the city's 12 bridges were incinerated. After crossing, Chamberlin collapsed on a lumber pile, so tired he no longer cared "whether the city stood or burned," and watched the Wells Street Bridge catch fire. One end burned faster than the other, making the unbalanced bridge tip and stand at a 60-degree angle in the water. The framework coursed with flame, like "a skeleton with ribs of fire," then "turned a complete somersault and plunged into the river." Anyone hoping to cross at Wells Street had to come up with another plan, and quickly. (The adventures of Alexander Frear, Joseph Edgar Chamberlin, and many others can be read in *The Great Chicago Fire in Eyewitness Accounts and 70 Contemporary Photographs and Illustrations*, compiled by David Lowe.)

CHECKMATE ON THE SOUTH SIDE

"It was broad day now," the *Chicago Post* wrote in their coverage of the fire. "At least, a small crimson ball hung in a pall of smoke, and people said that was the sun." In the early morning, the fire had doubled back to ingest all the big buildings it had missed, including the Chicago Tribune Building, the stores on Bookseller's Row, and Crosby's Opera House. The opera house had just been remodeled with a fortune in bronze statues and French upholstery, and it was scheduled to reopen the next night. A symphony orchestra that had been booked for the event pulled into 22nd Street Station just as the fire

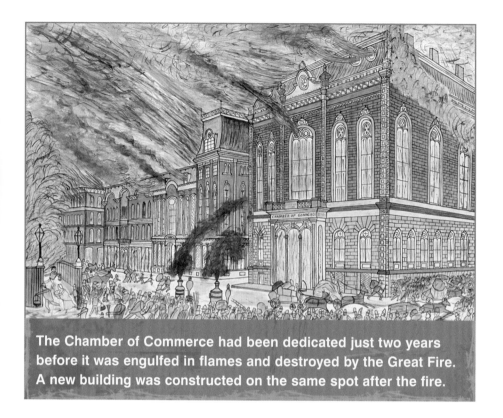

The Chamber of Commerce had been dedicated just two years before it was engulfed in flames and destroyed by the Great Fire. A new building was constructed on the same spot after the fire.

was reaching its peak. For one horrifying moment, the musicians stared at the fireball they had driven into, then pressed on to St. Louis.

At Harrison Street, along the southern edge of the fire, a number of small successes were adding up to a possible firebreak. The bleary-eyed firemen, who had been fighting since the Lull and Holmes Fire—36 hours without a decent sleep— had devised a scheme for relaying water from Lake Michigan. By placing several steamers in a line, they found they could pump water from one fire engine to the next and stretch their reach almost two blocks from the lakefront. At the same time, James Hildreth, the gunpowder enthusiast, had hit his stride and was blowing up a whole strip of homes on the north side of the street. Among other tricks, he had learned that if you shut two kegs of powder into a small closet, they explode with the force of five.

But when the tower of the Wabash Avenue Methodist Church caught flame, the dream of a firebreak was threatened. The church was a Gothic building at the corner of Harrison Street and Wabash, a critical location. The reverend had already spread sand on the floors and hung carpets soaked with lake water over the windows. But the ornamental tower was too high to reach, and when it began to smoke, the talk turned immediately to blowing it up. Hildreth placed five powder kegs in the church basement, while another Civil War veteran, General Sheridan, sent for six pieces of artillery to blast the tower to smithereens.

Just when it looked like the church was doomed, a quiet and unassuming man named William Haskell stepped out of the crowd. Haskell had also served in the Civil War, but more important, he had once been a professional gymnast.

"I think I can put that fire out," he said. "Please hold my coat."

Thousands of people watched as Haskell climbed a ladder 75 feet to the church roof, then made his way across the steeply pitched surface, pouring water from a bucket to cool his path and stopping occasionally to beat the embers from his clothes. Some of the bystanders lined up to form a long bucket brigade down to the lake and began passing pails of water for Haskell to pull up with a rope.

When Haskell reached the base of the rock tower, which soared 100 feet over the street, smoke was already pouring from the top. The chimneylike structure was burning from the inside. The gymnast soaked his clothes and wrapped a piece of wet cloth around his head like a bandana. He began his spidery ascent up the outside of the tower, clinging to the projecting rocks with his hands and feet, sometimes throwing the rope over a sharply jutting rock to haul himself up. Since his hands were no longer free to douse himself, his clothes began to smolder, wisps of steam rising off his tautly stretched muscles. Down below, the crowd held its breath, every face upturned.

When Haskell reached the top, he attached his rope to the tower—where he would later need it to bring up more water—and climbed down into the fiery interior. The crowd waited in silence for many tension-filled minutes. Just when it seemed certain that Haskell had perished, an arm appeared over the side of the tower, and then the gymnast himself emerged, his hair smoking and his clothes full of holes. But he did not stay long. He had only come to get another bucket of water, and in another moment, he ducked away again. He repeated this cycle again and again, until his body was black with soot, and every flame in the tower had been stilled. The church was finally saved.

With the church intact, it seemed clear that the fire would not travel farther south, and the crowds cheered the weary Haskell, dubbing him "Savior of the South Side." A basket was passed to collect money in appreciation, but Haskell never saw these funds. He went quietly home and never spoke of his feat, while the men who collected the cash secretly pocketed it.

But perhaps this is not so important. When everyday people perform selfless acts like Haskell's, it may be better to remember their courage than the thievery of the money collectors. Just as it may be better to remember the numerous wagon companies who drove refugees for free, rather than the drivers who overcharged, or the courageous tugboat captains who pulled burning ships to safety, rather than the frightened crowds who bumped people off the bridges. And what of men like Colonel Hough, who labored to chop his own house down, rather than allow it to fire the homes of his neighbors? Or the little girl who, while carrying two cats and a small dog, repeatedly urged her mother, "Don't cry mama," though she herself was sobbing. Such individual acts of generosity shone like jewels that terrible night. As Horace White, an editor of the *Chicago Tribune*, remarked:

> I saw a great many kindly acts done as we moved along. The poor helped the rich, and the rich helped the poor (if anybody could be called rich at such a time) to get on with their loads. I heard of cartmen demanding one hundred and fifty dollars (in hand, of course) for carrying a single load. Very likely it was so, but those cases did not come under my own notice. It did come under my notice that some cartmen worked for whatever the sufferers felt able to pay, and one I knew worked with alacrity for nothing. It takes all sorts of people to make a great fire.

6 North Side Holocaust

The North Side of Chicago was mostly residential, a broad expanse of stately homes owned by the city's oldest and richest families. There were a few businesses and some large clusters of modest, working-class cottages thrown into the mix, but overall, this district belonged to the wealthy. Imposing marble-faced mansions, their columns wrapped with ivy, loomed over the tree-lined avenues. Spread out behind many of these homes were beautiful gardens crossed by gravel paths, and the estate of at least one North Side resident, a previous mayor of the city, included an ice rink, a little billiard hall, and a fountain stocked with brook trout. At the same time, however, most of the streets were unpaved, and the presence of so much raw dirt, traversed by horses, goats, and other livestock, was a reminder of the humble country origins of even the city's most exclusive neighborhoods.

FASTER THAN A MAN COULD RUN

When the fire crossed to the North Side, most of its residents were asleep. They had grown bored with fires lately, and they would never have believed the flames could leap the main trunk of the river. Even Horace White, the editor of the *Tribune*, failed to heed his own newspaper's warnings of mass destruction. "I had retired to rest, though not to sleep, when the great bell struck the alarm," he recalls in Alfred T. Andreas's *History of Chicago*. "But fires had been so frequent of late, and had been so speedily extinguished, that I did not deem it worthwhile to get up and look at it, or even to count the strokes of the bell to learn where it was."

Many people woke to the explosive crash of the courthouse bell dropping from its tower, or the clattering of live coals on their roofs, or the banging of neighbors at their doors. In one neighborhood, everyone woke to the sound of a man on horseback, yelling, "Run for your lives! The fire has jumped the river!" As they stumbled from their homes in nightgowns and nightshirts (pajamas were not in fashion yet), they saw, in the near distance, a wall of red-hot air moving toward them. Most took steps to save their homes, soaking rugs in their cisterns and nailing them to the roof, or buried their valuables in the backyard. Some families even managed to dig pits deep enough to bury their pianos, though the scorching heat later baked these instruments to wire and ash.

Once the fire had a firm footing in the North Side, it burned with incredible speed, much faster than in the other two divisions. It was given wings by the broader streets, the more widely spaced homes, and the relentless leapfrogging of the firebrands, which worked like an advance guard to prime the streets ahead. The result was a blaze that was said to move faster than a man could run, and flames so loud that people only a few feet from each other had to shout to be heard. Within the homes, the intense heat melted the varnishes on furniture and made the walls smolder, causing black smoke to roll from the chimneys even before any flames had appeared. Once these houses reached the flash point and combusted, they "melted" in just a few minutes. George Payson, who lived on La Salle Street, recounts his attempts to save his home in Alfred T. Andreas's *History of Chicago*:

I made a feeble attempt to save the house. I knocked down the wooden steps that led up to the back door, and covered with blankets the doors that led down into the cellar. Having a bathtub full of water, I brought down a pailful to throw upon the blankets. As I opened the back door for that purpose, I saw the fire coming along the rear of the block with wonderful rapidity. A long arm of flame, seemingly without support, would dart out through the air; one touch of its finger and instantly the wooden balconies, fences, and outbuildings were in a blaze. A Lucifer match does not

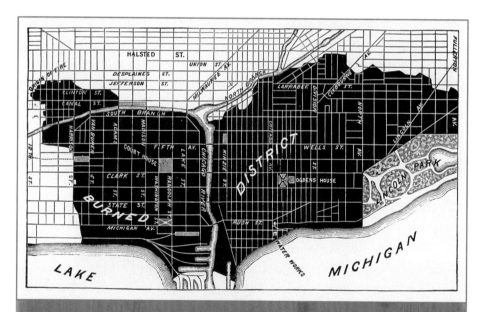

This map of Chicago highlights the areas burned in the great fire. While the fire started in Mrs. O'Leary's barn (located at the dot on the upper left-hand side), it continued right to the North Side, which suffered the most extensive damage. Many residents believed that the Chicago River would provide the boundary between their neighborhood and the fire, but the intensity of the fire and its debris managed to fly over the river and reach other parts of Chicago.

burn more quickly. Suddenly I received a blow in my face, as from some solid body, that almost knocked me off my feet. It was another burst of flame that came, I could not tell whence . . . I hastily closed the door, but the next moment it was bored through by the flames in a dozen places, as if it had been so much tissue paper. I saw then that this was the end of it. As the fire came into the house through the back, I ran out the front, into the burning street.

The northern streets were just as peopled as those of the other districts, though by most accounts, more eerily silent. The mass of refugees scarcely said a word as they struggled along with their bundles and trunks. They were awed, perhaps, by the scope of the sudden tragedy or focused on their struggles to breathe, since a dust storm accompanied the flames in this quarter. Their faces were black with soot, and they carried the usual assortment of disparate items: a caged canary, a marble clock, an armful of umbrellas. One little boy carried a landscape painting around his neck on a wire; the wire was too long, and the painting banged against his shins as he walked, making him cry.

When at last the whole strange parade had passed, the streets burned alone. There was no one left to watch as the skeleton frames of buildings fell to their knees, then pitched to the street with a shower of sparks. Only an occasional shirt or dress passed through this empty ghost town, floating down the street with arms outstretched.

The fire destroyed more buildings in the North Side than in the other two districts combined. In the West Side, for example, 500 buildings fell, and 2,250 people were left homeless. As the disaster picked up speed in the South Division, 3,650 buildings were destroyed, and 21,000 lost their homes. But in the North Side, the destruction was absolute. Out of 13,800 buildings, all but 500 were leveled, and 74,450 people were left with absolutely nothing and nowhere to live.

CHARLES AND FRENCHY

For the thousands of children trapped in the Great Chicago Fire, the experience was very traumatic but not without its brief moments of pleasure. John Healy, who was eight years old at the time, recalled his excitement at finding the streets littered with toys and the fun of loading his arms with all they could hold. Other children went to watch and cheer as their school caught fire. And one 14-year-old with a rifle stayed behind a few moments after his family had fled the house, then blasted all the French mirrors to pieces.

For 15-year-old Charles Anthony, the fire began as a great adventure. Robert Cromie recounts his story in *The Great Chicago Fire.*

Charles lived in a large estate with a garden full of peonies. Early in the fire, at around 11:00 P.M., he was woken by the family coach driver, who stood in the yard and threw pebbles at his window. Charles looked down into the yard. "Come on," whispered the coach driver, whose name was Frenchy. "There is a terrible fire down about the river."

Charles tiptoed out of the house, and he and Frenchy snuck away to one of the bridges, where the blaze was already consuming whole city blocks. After watching the fire awhile, they ran down to Lake Street, where someone said they could go into Hunt's hardware store and take whatever they wanted. The two ducked inside, and Frenchy took a rifle and a Colt revolver for himself, and a double-barreled shotgun for Charles. Frenchy wanted to go into a jewelry store next, but Charles talked him out of it. Instead, they joined a throng crossing through one of the tunnels. The tunnel was cluttered with furniture, and when they were halfway through, the crowd suddenly panicked and broke into a stampede. Young Charles was knocked to the ground twice, but both times Frenchy pulled him to his feet and saved him from being trampled.

After they burst gasping from the tunnel, a half-dressed woman stopped them and asked them to help rescue her sick

There were only a few safe locations that people could reach to escape the fire. Lincoln Park, the Sands, and even open prairies were filled with refugees and their belongings. Politicians and socialites huddled next to prostitutes and immigrants, as seen in this illustration, waiting for the fire to stop so they could return to the smoldering remains of their homes.

friend. Charles and Frenchy followed her to the second floor of a house, where they helped put the sick woman on a mattress and slide her down the stairs. The two then continued on their journey but soon decided that the fire was more terrifying than entertaining and that they had better bolt for home. As they ran, the drifting red flakes burned holes in Charles's coat, scalding his back, and singed his hair and eyebrows.

The Anthony family was very relieved to have Charles back, but there was little time to rejoice. All the household goods had to be buried in the backyard, and Charles had to release his chickens, guinea pigs, and rabbits to fend for themselves. Then Charles was given the assignment of making final adjustments to the doomed house. He shuttered the windows, closed the barn door, and came back around to the front gate. Just then an arc of flame swept over his head and broke all the windows on one side of the street, making him duck and run for his life.

After so many adult adventures, perhaps it was not surprising what happened a little later, when he tried to quench his thirst. "Charles was extremely thirsty," explains Cromie. "He entered a corner saloon and asked for a drink of water. The proprietor said there was none, but reached up and took a bottle from the shelf, broke off the neck, and poured a drink of whisky for Charles, the first he had ever tasted."

BAPTISM BY FIRE

One of the most elegant homes lost to the fire was that of writer and lawyer Isaac Arnold and his family. Arnold had been a friend of such historical figures as Abraham Lincoln, William Tecumseh Sherman, and Ulysses S. Grant, and his library was filled with thick volumes of their letters, along with 10,000 other books and some of the city's most valuable paintings. In addition to the huge mansion itself, the grounds were decked with greenhouses, summer homes, statuary, and two viner-ies. Old elm trees sat majestically on the lawns, with swaths of wild grapes and Virginia creeper hung between them. As visitors passed through the lilac hedges that surrounded this paradise, they were met by a babbling fountain and a sundial that said, "I number none but happy hours." As it turned out, these happy hours were numbered indeed.

When the red rain began falling against the night sky, Isaac Arnold led a nearly two-hour battle to try and save his property. There were two fire hydrants nearby, one in the front and one in the back of his house, and he hooked up hoses and stationed his servants across the grounds. Each time a pile of leaves or dead grass burst into flames, someone snuffed it out, but soon there were so many small fires that it was becoming harder and harder to keep up, and the servants were dashing about the lawns as if the fire were an Easter egg hunt. As Andreas reports:

> Every moment, the contest grew warmer, and more desperate, until, by three o'clock, the defenders of the castle were becoming seriously exhausted. At the hour mentioned, [thirteen-year-old] Arthur Arnold called to his father, "The barn and hay are on fire!" "The leaves are on fire on the east side!" said the gardener. "The front piazza is in a blaze!" cried another. "The front greenhouse is in flames!" "The roof is on fire!" "The water has stopped!" was the last appalling announcement. "Now, for the first time," said Mr. Arnold, "I gave up all hope of saving my home . . ."

At that point, Isaac Arnold was faced with a frightening dilemma. He and his family were surrounded to the south, west, and north by towering cliffs of flame. The only direction to run was eastward to the Sands, a little strip of beach where the lakeshore met the river. So that was exactly where they went.

Like Conley's Patch, the Sands had once been a seedy strip of gambling shanties and brothels, but 20 years earlier, the city had torn down all these dubious shacks, leaving only a sandy beach. As the Sun came up on Monday morning, October 9, 1871, the Sands were the setting of more human misery than they had ever known in their glory days. The beach was entirely filled with thousands of refugees and braying animals. The rich and poor huddled together amid piles of furniture, clutching their final possessions, while thieves kicked open the trunks and took whatever they wanted. Invalids lay moaning on feather mattresses, and crying children clung to their mothers' necks. One little girl carried a cage with a pet canary and wept when the bird finally tumbled down dead from its perch.

As bad as things were on the beach, they got worse when the lumberyards south of the Sands took fire. This blaze released mountains of smoke and embers, which poured across the Sands, lighting the furniture and nearly suffocating the crowds. As Del Moore wrote in a letter to her parents, "The sun disappeared, the wind increased, straw blew, feather beds and blankets blazed and even the people were on fire. . . . For the only time unmitigated fear took possession of me. I begged [my husband] if I took fire to put me in the Lake and drown me, not let me burn to death."

Del Moore was not the only one who felt this way. With literally nowhere left to go but the water, people made their final exodus, fleeing into the chill embrace of Lake Michigan. Parents waded in as deep as possible while still holding their children aloft, while others ran in up to their necks and turned their backs to the fire, trying gingerly to breathe the scorching air. Those who had horses rode them as far into the water as they would go and waited on their backs. Wagons, trunks, and even sofas were dragged into the lake as perches. But getting out into the lake was only the beginning of this long and often agonizing vigil. It was a struggle to breathe and to endure the cold of the water and the heat of the air. Hissing firebrands fell thickly and steadily, constantly threatening every exposed part of the body. Many people ended up waiting like this for more than 10 hours—all morning, all afternoon, and part of the evening—while the millions of feet of lumber burned away.

Not content to stand all day in the lake, Isaac Arnold tried a different strategy. He led his children along the edge of the water to a stone pier. With much difficulty, they managed to make it down the pier to a wooden rowboat, and then, with Arnold rowing, to a lighthouse that stood nearby. Inside the lighthouse, they met a handful of others who had had the same idea, including a bank cashier with a trunk containing $1.6 million in cash and securities. The group waited inside the lighthouse for several hours, unsure what to do next. The fragile structure was continuously threatened by burning boats that drifted on the river and by the roaring flames blowing out from the shore. Eventually even the pier began to burn. Around 4:00 P.M., a fire-blistered tugboat tied up near the lighthouse, and the group decided to seize the opportunity. With $1.6 million on hand, they were able to offer the captain a huge pile of cash to take them aboard and carry them through the fire to the West Side.

In preparation for their trip, they fed the engine till it had a full head of steam, and then they hooked a hose up to the pumps so they could put out fires on the deck. The women and children went down to the pilot house and shut the portholes tight, while the men crouched behind the bulwarks. The captain took the wheel, and they began to run the gauntlet of fire. The prow of the boat was carefully threaded past the hulks of fallen bridges and the logjams of burning timber. Flames shot like torches from the grain elevators on either shore, and coils of smoke rolled across the decks. Finally the superheated air began to tax the engine, making it groan and strain. The pumps gave out, leaving no water to smother the fires that kept springing up on the decks. There were cries to turn back, but it was too late for that now. As the cinders grew thicker, Arnold

CORNER
STATE & MADISON ST
AFTER CHICAGO FIRE

After the fire was extinguished, the full extent of the damage was evident. Homes and businesses were destroyed, and many refugees who could not carry any belongings with them were left with nothing. Here, a photograph of the intersection at State and Madison Streets, in Chicago's city center, shows the ruins of the fire.

pushed his son down on the deck and covered his head with a wet handkerchief, then helped the men put out fires with their coats. At last the tugboat chugged past its final obstacle—a tangle of wood and iron that had once been the Wells Street Bridge. The smoke lifted away, and the air grew clear and cool. Everyone watched in silence as the flames began to recede into the distance. Arnold looked over at the captain, an expression of relief and gratitude on his face. "We are through, sir," the captain said.

"ISN'T THIS THE LAST DAY?"

Not everyone in the North Side escaped to the Sands. Tens of thousands escaped north to Lincoln Park, a forested area that contained several lakes and a cemetery. The cemetery was in the process of being relocated, and families took shelter in the open graves or behind stacks of gravestones. Those who had towed their belongings to this distant site were soon disappointed, since the heaps of furniture caught fire here too, forcing the homeless to break camp once again and move deeper into the wilderness.

Thousands of others ran west to the open prairies, where they collapsed of exhaustion in the dirt. According to A.S. Chapman, who was a seven-year-old boy at the time, "The cows were gone from the prairie. In their place was a scene of indescribable chaos—piles of clothing and furniture—buggies, carts and wagons—people moving restlessly among them—mothers holding back their own tears to comfort their children—the contents of a thousand homes emptied on the raw prairie with the only thought of escape. There [my schoolteacher] and I waited and watched the ring of fire draw nearer." Even on the prairie, the Great Chicago Fire showed no mercy. After a little break, it lit the prairie grasses and sent everyone fleeing west again. "I had to wake the children up," wrote Julia Lemos, a widow with five children, "and we had to run again, and leave everything to burn, this time we felt the heat on our backs when we ran, like when one stands with the back to a grate fire. . . ." After shepherding her children to a safer location, she rested on the grass with her son Willie's head in her lap.

"Willie, Mother is here," she said. "Don't cry."

"Yes, but Mama," the child asked between sniffles, "Isn't this the Last Day?"

It may well have seemed like it, and in fact, for an estimated 300 people, it was. Most of these deaths took place in Conley's Patch, and on Chicago Avenue in the North Side, which became a claustrophobic dead end when the Chicago Street Bridge closed. Some died leaping from burning buildings, others were crushed under falling walls, and at least one little girl drowned in the river after being forced off the bridge by the crowds. Charred corpses were also found at the foot of Chatfield Bridge, which had been turned on its side by a burning ship. One man, who worked as a janitor at the historical society building, died after helping to try and save the Emancipation Proclamation. Lincoln's executive order freeing the slaves had been enacted only eight years earlier, during the height of the Civil War, but was already one of the country's most treasured historical documents. The janitor and another man removed it from its case and wrapped it in flags, but when explosions rocked the historical society, they dropped it, along with Lincoln's walking stick, and fled empty-handed. Two days later, the janitor's body was found on a nearby street.

There was no real way to count the number of dead, since in many places the fire acted as a crematorium, incinerating even the bones of the corpses. But the body count was certainly lower than expected for such a deadly tempest. The wide, straight, and level avenues were partly to thank for this. They made the evacuation much swifter and less complicated than would have been possible on narrower or hillier thoroughfares. And there was also an element of blind luck, or perhaps providence, in the relative lack of casualties. One three-month-old baby was found, by a policeman, lying on the pavement. She had been stripped from her mother's arms by the sheer pressure of the crowd, which then swept the poor woman along, deaf to her cries for the fallen child. The child was hungry but otherwise okay.

Out on the prairie, as families huddled in silence, another small miracle occurred. It was nearly midnight, and everyone was afraid the wind would shift, causing the fire to destroy the remainder of the West Side. But the change they felt in the air was of a different type. It was a drizzling, cold rain. All across the blackened city, people held out their palms and looked to the sky in disbelief. It seemed too good to be true, but there could be no denying it: That was water streaking

The Poor Get Poorer

At the time of the Great Fire, the distribution of Chicago's wealth was extremely uneven. As described in *Smoldering City* by Karen Sawislak, if you were to split the population into two parts, with one part being the wealthier half and the other part being the poorer half, the poorer half would have controlled only one percent of the city's wealth, leaving 99 percent for the other half! There is no question that the poor suffered the most during the fire. Most of the fatalities occurred in the tightly packed slums. In addition, many of the poor were unable to pay the exorbitant wagon fees to rescue their belongings, did not have high-paying jobs that would allow them to rebuild their lives, and did not have wealthy friends elsewhere in the city to take them in. While the rich went away to their lake houses in Wisconsin, many of the poor had to resort to sleeping under bridges. Patrick Web, a day laborer, lamented the situation: "I felt broken down in spirits, seeing all that I had saved during my life (about $1500) by hard labor, honesty and sobriety, swept away in a few hours, and I at the age of fifty-eight."

down their ash-covered faces. As they watched and waited, the drops grew faster and bolder. By 3:00 A.M., a steady curtain of rain was pouring down, slicing its way through the ceiling of gray smoke. The drought of three months, and the horror of the last 24 hours, were over. In a letter written to her mother, a North Side resident named Mary Fales captured the sentiment perfectly: "I never felt so grateful in all my life as to hear the rain pour down."

7 City in a Hurry Again

As the Sun rose on Tuesday morning, thousands of Chicagoans staggered back into their blackened city, trying in vain to find their old streets and neighborhoods. The cityscape had been completely transformed into a ghostly field of black, lined with the shapes of partially devoured walls. Most of the homes were reduced to giant holes that had once been their basements. Pale-blue coal fires continued to flicker at the bottom of these cavities, while in the yards a few blackened trees remained, their tortured branches frozen in the direction of the previous night's wind.

As the refugees moved across this eerie wasteland, they had to pick their way over tons of rubble. Bricks lay in crumbled heaps, iron pipes were melted into shapeless blobs, and marble blocks were turned to mounds of powder. The terrible heat had even pulled some of the railroad tracks out of the ground and left them sticking in the air like signposts.

In all, 73 miles of streets and 17,500 buildings were destroyed. The number of people left homeless was 100,000—nearly one-third the total population of the city. Astonishingly, only about 300 people were killed, the majority from the crowded slums and shantytowns. Most of these bodies were incinerated beyond recognition, but about 70 corpses were carried to a horse stable and lined up in rows on the dirt floor. Thousands of people visited this temporary morgue, terrified they would recognize the body of one of their missing loved ones. One visitor, historian Frank Luzerne, later described one of the corpses:

> The next was the body of a young man partially clad in common workingman's attire. The hair was completely burned off his head and body; the features were blackened and distorted with pain; the swollen lips were wide apart, disclosing the glistening teeth, and imparting a horrid grin, such only as agonizing death can stamp upon the face. The flesh was bloated to an astonishing size. The poor wretch was roasted alive. (This account can be read in *The Great Fire* by Jim Murphy.)

To prevent more deaths, some basic human needs had to be met right away. The most pressing requirements were food and water. The water shortage brought on by the destruction of the Waterworks was solved in the short run by pumping water out of the river. People who tasted it said this water was "smoky but good," but unfortunately, it was also unsanitary, and an epidemic of typhoid soon broke out in the city. It was not until several weeks later that one of the Waterworks engines was finally repaired, and the city had a steady source of clean water.

As for food, it began to flow into the city by train as early as Tuesday evening. "Barrels and boxes came pouring in, filled with cooked hams, roasts of beef, pork, veal, turkeys, chickens, and indeed everything in the way of meat and bread," reported a relief worker in Alfred Andreas's *History of Chicago*. Other train cars were loaded full of coats, shoes, and underwear, along with blankets, mattresses, and medical supplies. These

Refugees with nothing left received donations from people all across America. Clothing, food, and water were provided to those who had nowhere to go, as seen here, and a large amount of money was raised to help the victims. An estimated 100,000 people were left homeless by the fire.

donations came from all across America, since the whole country had been following Chicago's fiery drama through the telegraph wires. Everyone knew about it, and everyone wanted to help. In fact, people were so eager to contribute that when the relief trains passed through their towns, they tried to throw bundles onto the cars.

In addition, nearly $4 million was raised, a tremendous amount at the time. Major American cities contributed, along with 29 foreign countries. Smaller groups gathered their spare change, like the crew of the U.S.S. *Vermont*, who gave a day of their pay, and the paperboys of Cincinnati, who gave two days of theirs. The army loaned 50,000 tents, which were immediately pitched to house the poor. And two prominent Englishmen began to collect books for a Chicago public library, with everyone from the United Kingdom's Queen Victoria to Prime Minister Benjamin Disraeli contributing volumes from their personal collections.

The mayor gave the Chicago Relief and Aid Society the job of collecting and distributing all these charitable donations. He also issued several proclamations. One of them forbid saloons from selling liquor until further notice, and another made it illegal to smoke in the street. A third tried to address the presumed cause of the fire, expressly forbidding the use of kerosene lamps in barns. It is a wonder Catherine O'Leary was not made to write this proclamation 99 times, so demonized had she become, already, for her unconfirmed role in the fire.

Public Library

A group of English writers and politicians, including Alfred, Lord Tennyson; Robert Browning; John Stuart Mill; and Queen Victoria donated a collection of books for the creation of a new public library. The donors thought Chicago had lost its library during the fire, but the truth was, Chicago had never had a public library. Rather than admit this embarrassing fact, the city decided to start one, so they fitted the inside of an old water tank with gas lights, tables, and circular shelves and replaced the top with a skylight. Although it was primitive, at least this library was fireproof.

SEND COFFEE. DON'T CRY.

The awesome courage with which Chicagoans picked themselves up and started over became the stuff of legend. There was a sense that the second coming of Chicago was inevitable, that the city was an almost supernatural force that could not be stopped. The metaphor that was frequently used was that of the phoenix, the mythical bird that burned itself up in a funeral pyre, then rose from its own ashes in triumphant rebirth. Three days after the fire, Joseph Medill wrote an editorial that captured the general desire for transcendence:

> All is not lost. Though four hundred million dollars worth
> of property has been destroyed, Chicago still exists. She was
> not a mere collection of stones, and bricks, and lumber. . .
> The great natural resources are all in existence: the lake . . .
> the spacious harbor, the vast empire of production extend-
> ing westward to the Pacific . . . the great arteries of trade
> and commerce, all remain unimpaired, undiminished, and
> all ready for immediate resumption. . . . We have lost money,
> but we have saved life, health, vigor and industry. . . . Let
> the Watchword henceforth be: *Chicago Shall Rise Again.*
> (This editorial appeared in the *Chicago Tribune* and, later,
> in Robert Cromie's *The Great Chicago Fire.*)

Displaying the same hopeful pluck, the city's masters of commerce—its businessmen, and salespeople, its wheelers and dealers and hucksters—began to dust themselves off and plot new ways to make money. It was said that, even before the fire was out, builders were out feeling the bricks to see if they were cool enough to be used again. On Tuesday morning, Margaret O'Toole opened her chestnut stand amid the piles of charred, smoking wreckage and earned herself a place in history as the first person to open for business. Soon after, a real estate agent named William Kerfoot nailed together a little shack and hung up a sign that captured the prevailing sentiment: "W.D. Kerfoot Real Estate. All Gone but Wife, Children, and Energy."

The Western Union telegraph office set up that same morning, using a brick warehouse as an office and wooden boards set on barrels as a countertop. People lined up for a block and a half to send telegrams. One of the first was a telegram from a local merchant to his wife, who was away in New York at the time of the fire:

STORE AND CONTENTS, DWELLING AND EVERY-
THING LOST. INSURANCE WORTHLESS. SEE __
IMMEDIATELY; TELL HIM TO BUY ALL THE COF-
FEE HE CAN AND SHIP THIS AFTERNOON BY
EXPRESS. DON'T CRY.

Other businesses packed themselves into houses just outside the fire district. A typical house had a shoe store in the basement, a button factory on the first floor, offices for doctors

Lieutenant Philip Sheridan, seen here, was put in charge of maintaining order in Chicago with the use of the military, the police, and a volunteer force. He oversaw two weeks of martial law in the city, which was met with general public uproar. Martial law ended after a volunteer shot and killed a man.

and lawyers in the bedrooms, and a telegraph office in the attic. Down on the streets, children set up tables and sold fire souvenirs, such as melted together pieces of silverware.

The newspapers had perhaps the greatest incentive to recover quickly, since the story of a lifetime was unfolding before them. The editors of the *Chicago Tribune* quickly rented a little printing shop in a safe part of town. There was no steam printing press, and the only pieces of printing type were capital letters and numbers, but the shop was better than nothing. On Tuesday afternoon, they borrowed brooms to sweep it up, and money to buy stoves. One of their first visitors was a man carrying a paintbrush. "I haven't a morsel of food for my wife and children tonight," he said, "and not a cent to buy any; may I paint '*Tribune*' over your door?" The editors agreed, and paid the man $3.75 for his efforts.

Now the *Tribune* had a sign, and with a sign came a source of income, as people began to line up outside to place personal advertisements. These ads were one of the main ways that families with lost children could find them again, which was very important, because in the days after the fire, some 2,000 children were wandering about looking for their parents. The first sheet of personals read, in part, as follows:

> Mrs. Tinney lost little girl six years old, Katie, Harrison House.
> James Glass lost little boy, Arthur Glass, 342 Hubbard Street.
> A little girl, cannot speak her name, at Desplaines Hotel.
> Henry Schneider, baby, in blue poland waist, red skirt, has white hair.
> Mr. McLogan, 288 Laflin, has a boy 2 or 3 years old— speaks French.

Another important business helping Chicago regain its footing was the hotel industry. Hotels were needed to house the

Bank Vaults

After the fire, the banks had to wait several days to see if the money inside their vaults was intact. If they opened their safes and vaults too soon, the sudden contact with oxygen would make the superheated currency burst into flames. So they tried to be patient and to conscript the fire department into spraying their safes with water. The vaults were finally opened on Friday and Saturday, and the contents of a few of the smaller ones did indeed burst into flame. But the vast majority of the cash was all right, and the bank officers—not to mention everyone with a savings account—breathed a huge sigh of relief.

wealthier citizens, as well as for the tourists and investors the city desperately hoped to attract.

Of all the hotel owners trying to get up and running again, surely none had the luck of John Drake. Drake was the owner of the Tremont House, the elegant hotel that had burned to the ground three times. Several nights earlier, at the height of the Great Chicago Fire, Drake was running away from the flaming ruins of his hotel when he had a strange impulse. He decided to duck into another hotel, the Michigan Avenue Hotel, which was directly in the path of the approaching fire. The lobby was filled with frightened, yelling guests, but he managed to push past them and find the owner. The owner asked what he wanted, and Drake said he wanted to buy the hotel. He even took $1,000 out of his pocket as a down payment. The owner looked at Drake like he was crazy. Did he not understand that the building was about to be wrapped in flames? But Drake insisted he was serious, and so, as the guests jostled past with their luggage, the two men wrote out a bill of sale and signed it. As Drake left the hotel, the owner shouted after him: "This building will go next," he said, pointing to the flames pouring from a nearby roof.

But the building did not go next. This happened to be the part of town where the fire engines were still at work, pumping water in a relay up from the lake, and where explosives were used to create a firebreak. The fire was stopped just before reaching the hotel, and John Drake's gamble paid off.

A week later, Drake returned to the hotel, but the owner refused to acknowledge their deal. Drake left and came back with a group of tall, muscular friends. He set his pocket watch on a table and gave the owner of the Michigan Avenue Hotel exactly five minutes to agree to their deal or else. This did the trick. "Drake renamed his hotel the Tremont House after the ruined building," wrote historian Donald Miller, "and it became a local landmark, marking the southern boundary of the fire, and a symbol of the city's amazing recovery from one of the greatest disasters of modern times."

BOOMTOWN

Recycling unburned buildings and packing businesses into people's homes would not be enough to restore Chicago to its former greatness. If the city was going to truly recover, the thousands of lost buildings had to be replaced. And this had to be done quickly, because there was a danger that Chicago would lose much of its business to other midwestern cities, such as St. Louis and Milwaukee. At the same time, the traumatized Chicagoans needed a project to throw themselves into, something that would tap their skills and take their minds off their losses. The solution to all these problems was to revive the myth that had defined Chicago from the very beginning, the myth of a city grown overnight as if built by elves. The story of the sudden birth of Chicago was a story that

The destruction of the city and the threat of losing businesses to other Midwestern cities spurred rapid recovery and growth in Chicago. Buildings and hotels were quickly rebuilt, as seen *(above)* in a photo taken a year after the fire, and makeshift houses were constructed to temporarily house the homeless. Despite the wooden buildings being one of the main causes of the fire's ferocity, builders believed they needed to act quickly and, once again, used lumber as their primary construction material.

was integral to the city's self-esteem, and it was a narrative its depressed citizens needed to tell again after the fire.

Over the next two years, Chicago would embark on a rebuilding project that was like a mirror image of its initial boom. The builders did not waste any time getting started. In fact, the last house burned to the ground Tuesday morning, and the first shipment of lumber arrived Tuesday afternoon. In less than two months, 5,000 wooden shanties were built across the city as single-family dwellings, and crude barracks were thrown up to shelter the poor through the winter. At the same time, workers were erecting thousands of larger wooden-frame buildings. All the fire rubble was carted down to the lake and thrown in the water, creating a five-acre landfill that would later become part of Grant Park. Historian Alfred T. Andreas observed the building frenzy with amazement: "It is common to see ten or a dozen or fifty houses rising at once; but when one looks upon, not a dozen or fifty, but upon *ten thousand* houses rising and ten times that number of busy workmen coming and going, and listens to the noise of countless saws and hammers and chisels and axes and planes, he is bewildered."

It might be expected that the city planners would heed the lessons of the Great Fire and finally insist on more fire-resistant construction. Amazingly, this was not the case. Wood was the principle material of the two-year building boom, and the lessons of the Great Fire were mostly ignored. "Speed was thought more important than deliberation," explained Ross Miller in his book *American Apocalypse.* "Architectural quality was less important than the psychological function of allowing people to forget." Often, construction on a building would begin even before the plans were finished. The result was an uncanny facsimile of the city that had burned so eagerly in October 1871. William Croffut, an editor of the *Chicago Evening Post*, looked out over the resurrected Chicago one year after the fire and made a grave pronouncement:

> The gravest peril of the city now lies in the prolonged existence and ceaseless multiplication of these combustible piles of lumber. Fire limits were prescribed by a timid Common Council in the hour of its dissolution, but the ordinance is openly violated in every part of the city with perfect impunity. . . . It would seem that Chicago could

scarcely afford an encore of the performance of October 8 and 9; but a repetition of that tragedy is [certain] to follow the persistence in our clapboard and shingle madness . . . (William Croffut's testimony can be read in *The Great Chicago Fire in Eyewitness Accounts and 70 Contemporary Photographs and Illustrations*, edited by David Lowe.)

After two years of frantic building, an unexpected event woke the city from its dangerous, repetitive dream. In 1873, a bank failure in New York led to a financial crisis known as the Panic of 1873, which ushered in a six-year period of economic depression. Thus, for the entire second half of the 1870s, building completely stopped in Chicago, and the city was able to catch its breath and think about its future. As if to encourage careful reflection, a fire known as The Little Fire broke out in 1874, ripping across the same old wooden sidewalks and tar roofs and destroying a dozen blocks downtown.

When the depression finally ended in 1879, the architects rolled up their sleeves once again, and the building derricks slowly lifted their necks above the city. It was time for the second phase of rebuilding, and this time, things would be different.

8 Nowhere to Go but Up

"It all started in the long grass of the prairies," said Frank Lloyd Wright, the great American architect. He was talking about the skyscraper, the new invention that would remake Chicago, giving birth to the vertical city we know today. In the decade after the Great Fire, the skyscraper was elevated to an art form in Chicago, and it transformed the once rustic prairie town into the birthplace of modern architecture.

AMERICA'S CITY

When the financial crisis of the 1870s ended, Chicago was ready to start building again. But most of the land downtown was already developed, and since the city had water on three sides, and a web of railroad terminals on the fourth, there was nowhere else to go but straight up toward the clouds. A new invention called the skyscraper made this possible.

The steel-frame skyscraper was an ingenious idea, the most important architectural breakthrough since the cathedral. Before the invention of the modern skyscraper, the walls of a building were load-bearing—that is, they had to support the building's weight. But in the skyscraper, a steel frame supported all the weight, and the walls were simply hung on the frame like curtains. Because they no longer had to support the weight of the building, the walls could be very thin and light. This, in turn, meant that many more floors could be added, along with vast glass windows that previously would have shattered under the weight of the building.

The skyscraper found its greatest expression in Chicago in the 1880s and 1890s. It was over this period that architects such as William Le Baron Jenney, John Wellborn Root, and Louis H. Sullivan created a new style of architecture called the Chicago School. Their skyscrapers had a simple clarity that was breathtakingly new. All the gaudy ornamentation of the old buildings had been stripped away, leaving only clean, flat planes that seemed to soar into the air as serenely as birds. The skyscrapers of the Chicago School did not pretend to be made of marble or to be beautiful cathedrals or Greek temples. They proudly advertised what they were: steel-framed towers built for conducting business and making money. To see them was to understand their structure and function in an instant. It was as if the city had finally embraced its own commerce-driven history and in doing so had found its integrity and inner beauty.

One by one, the postfire buildings were replaced with sky-scrapers, and the Chicago we know today, the towering city of steel and glass on the bank of Lake Michigan, gradually began to crystallize. "People began calling it America's City," wrote historian Donald Miller, "'the concentrated essence of Americanism.' Foreign writers, especially, saw this raw unfinished colossus, with its surging commercial energy, technological wonders, and absence of settled traditions as the most characteristically American of America's largest cities. Older eastern cities like Boston, New York, and Philadelphia reminded the French architecture critic Jacques Hermant of 'the great English cities,' while San Francisco had 'a Spanish or Chinese flavor.' But 'Chicago,' he declared, 'is America.'"

During the great rebuilding, Americans continued to pour into the promising new city, its rebirth calling to them like a beacon of hope. *Chicago Tribune* editor William Bross famously predicted that Chicago would reach a population of one million by 1900. In fact, the city broke the one-million barrier in 1890, surpassing Philadelphia to become the second-largest city in America.

NEVER AGAIN

There was another big advantage to skyscrapers. They were such expensive building projects that investors and insurance companies would not fund and insure them unless they were truly fireproof. So architects developed new innovations to

The need for rebuilding in Chicago provided great opportunities for the unemployed architect Louis H. Sullivan *(left)*, who moved to the Windy City from Philadelphia. Sullivan's work had a great impact on American architecture.

make them safe—placing water tanks on the roofs, installing fire hoses on each floor, and mounting chemical fire extinguishers and automatic sprinkler systems in the hallways.

Then there were the new materials themselves—steel and glass—which were more fire resistant than wood. Even iron beams, which had melted in the Great Fire, were no longer a problem, thanks to a technique inspired by an architect named John Van Osdel. During the Great Fire, Van Osdel had tried to preserve some of his blueprints by burying them in a pit in his basement and covering them with layers of sand and clay. When he returned after the fire, he found that the clay had formed a protective layer, just as he had hoped, leaving his blueprints unharmed. This gave engineers the idea of covering iron beams with tiny squares of terra-cotta, the clay used in flowerpots. In the event of fire, the clay would insulate the beams, protecting them just like the papers in Van Osdel's basement.

Other city improvements reinforced the architectural changes. For example, the wooden roads and sidewalks were gradually replaced with brick and stone. The fire department was completely reorganized in a military fashion, with the fire companies separated into 18 battalions like an army. A Chicago fireman invented the fire pole to help his fellow firefighters drop to their engines more quickly. And over the next several decades, the steam-driven fire engines were replaced with motorized ones, which were faster and more reliable.

One hugely important change was that the city finally purchased a Holly Fire Protection System. The Holly System had already been adopted by hundreds of cities around the world, but Chicago had deemed it too expensive. As with other cost-cutting measures taken by the city council, the system might have greatly limited the damage from the Great Fire. The idea behind the Holly System was simple. Centralized steam engines and rotary water pumps were used to maintain a high level of pressure in the hydrant lines, so the fire engines did not have to generate their own water pressure. All a fire engine had to do was connect to a hydrant, and the water shot out.

Improvements in fire prevention and firefighting have continued over the more than 100 years since the Great Fire. Many of these changes are stressed during Fire Prevention Week, a national event that takes place each year during the week of October 7, in commemoration of that fateful day in 1871.

THE DECLINE OF CATHERINE O'LEARY

Strangely enough, the little house of Patrick and Catherine O'Leary was still standing after the Great Fire. Their barn, of course, had been the first structure to fall, but then the fire headed north and east. The irony of their house being spared was wasted on no one, and the newspapers quickly picked up on it, adding it to the broader narrative of the O'Leary's guilt. The *New York Tribune* sneered, "There it stood safe, while a city had perished before it and around it. . . . And there to this hour stands that craven little house, holding on tightly to its miserable existence."

However, despite its derisive tone, at least this report was basically true—the house was, in fact, still standing. This may have been one of the only accurate things ever written about poor Catherine O'Leary. When the newspapers seized on the rumor of her starting the fire, they were only getting started. The *Chicago Times* gleefully described her as a 70-year old "hag" with a doubled-over back, although in fact she was a healthy woman in her early forties. And even though she and her husband were hard workers raising five children and holding several jobs at once, they were described as ignorant, drunken immigrants who were cheating the city to receive welfare. In fact, the newspapers took the welfare story one step further, claiming that when the city finally stopped Mrs. O'Leary's welfare payments, she started the fire to get even. "The old hag swore she would be revenged on a city that would deny her a bit of wood or a pound of bacon," wrote the *Chicago Times*.

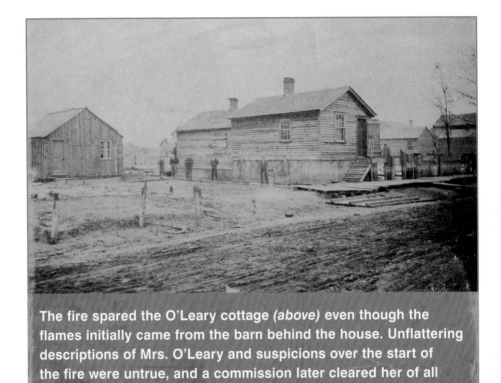

The fire spared the O'Leary cottage *(above)* even though the flames initially came from the barn behind the house. Unflattering descriptions of Mrs. O'Leary and suspicions over the start of the fire were untrue, and a commission later cleared her of all charges in 1997.

This kind of language is very revealing about the true reason for the O'Learys' maltreatment. There was at the time (and still is today) a tendency to fear and blame the poor. The underprivileged in general—and immigrants in particular—were seen as being dangerous, chaotic, lazy, drunken, and often criminal. Thus, for example, while the wealthy Chicagoans were generally depicted as evacuating the city in an orderly fashion during the fire, the poor were often described as behaving like animals. The *Chicago Evening Post* gave this description of a slum during the fire:

> Villainous, haggard with debauch and pinched with misery, flitted through the crowd collarless, ragged, dirty, unkempt, these negroes with stolid faces and white men

who fatten on the wages of shame, glided through the masses like vultures in search of prey. They smashed windows reckless of the severe wounds inflicted on their naked hands, and with bloody fingers rifled impartially till, shelf and cellar, fighting viciously for the spoils of their forays. Women, hollow-eyed and brazen-faced, with foul drapery tied over their heads, their dresses half torn from their skinny bosoms, and their feet thrust into trodden down slippers, moved here and there, stealing, scolding shrilly, and laughing with one another at some particularly "splendid" gush of flame or "beautiful" falling in of a roof.

It seems hard to imagine that anyone believed such exaggerated reporting, but unfortunately, they did. They believed it because it fit with things they already imagined were true about the immigrant and working classes. And because of such prejudices, it became easy to blame the entire event on the poor. After all, people reasoned, had the fire not taken hold in the cluttered shantytowns where the poor people lived? And while this was certainly true, it was also true that lumberyards and other businesses played a major role in spreading the fire and that the wood-encrusted hotels and banks in the heart of the city burned just as readily as the working-class cottages. In fact, it was the way the entire city was constructed that fueled the fire. In addition, the city council repeatedly refused to give the fire marshal the equipment he needed. This last problem may have been the most important factor of all, according to an inquiry conducted after the fire. For example, if Fire Chief Williams had only been given the two fireboats he had repeatedly requested, the fire would never have crossed the river.

In any case, as a poor Irish woman, Catherine O'Leary was a natural scapegoat. After the fire her house was assailed with reporters and tourists, all of them hoping to catch a glimpse of the drunken milk lady with the broken lantern. Although she refused all interviews, Catherine O'Leary could not get peace. She and her family had to abandon their infamous address, moving to a series of different homes before finally settling on Halsted Street on the South Side. For the rest of her life, she refused to talk about the fire or to capitalize on her notoriety in any way, rejecting the stream of offers from the likes of P.T. Barnum, who wanted her to tour with his circus, or the Chicago Fire Cyclorama, which simply wanted to buy her endorsement. She became a recluse, leaving her house only for small errands or to go to morning Mass.

But the lifetime of badgering and abuse took their toll. Her physician, Dr. Swayne Wickersham, commented in an interview in 1894, "It would be impossible for me to describe to you the grief and indignation with which Mrs. O'Leary views the place that has been assigned her in history. That she is regarded as the cause, even accidentally, of the Great Chicago Fire is the grief of her life." In September 1894, 23 years after the fire, Patrick O'Leary collapsed on his doorstep and died. Catherine followed 10 months later, ostensibly as the result of pneumonia, though her neighbors said she died of a broken heart.

Mrs. O'Leary and the Paparazzi

For the rest of her life, Catherine O'Leary managed to evade every paparazzo who popped up beside her with a camera. To this day, we have no real likeness of her, although scores of fake ones were published. In one typical postcard, a squat, angry-looking woman poses behind what is meant to be Mrs. O'Leary's cow, but is actually a bull.

THE TRUTH?

In 1997, Richard Bales, a historian with a flair for detective work, reexamined the case of Mrs. O'Leary and the start of the Great Chicago Fire. After an exhaustive, six-year investigation of every aspect of the moments before the fire began, he was able to put to rest, once and for all, the legend of the

By the early 1900s, Chicago's streetscapes had changed drastically. The advent of skyscrapers and more modern, durable construction materials rendered the city almost unrecognizable in places, including the bustling State Street *(above)*.

cow, the lantern, and the late-night milking. Like the Board of Police and Fire Commissioners before him, but with much more effective reasoning, he found Mrs. O'Leary not guilty. One of the simplest proofs of her innocence was that she had no insurance on the barn. Had she started the fire, she would have instantly realized that her livelihood—her five cows, her horse, and her calf—were about to be destroyed. She could not have known, at first, that the fire would be any larger than other recent blazes in the city, so there would have been no reason for her to conceal her role in starting it. Thus she would have done what anyone does after accidentally starting their property on fire. She would have tried to put the fire out, and failing that, she would have called for help.

And indeed, someone did try to stomp out the fire in the barn, and someone did call for help, but it was not Mrs. O'Leary. It was Daniel "Peg Leg" Sullivan, the young man who claimed to have been sitting across the street when flames popped through the barn roof.

Using old photos, real estate records, testimony from the fire inquiry, and numerous histories and documents, Richard Bales showed that the testimony given by Peg Leg Sullivan to the Board of Police and Fire Commissioners was riddled with holes. For example, by painstakingly reconstructing the positions of all the buildings on DeKoven Street, he showed that Sullivan could not actually have seen the roof of the O'Leary barn from where he claimed to have been sitting. Through this and other proofs, Bales concluded that it was Sullivan himself who started the fire. The one-legged drayman, perhaps accompanied by his friend Dennis Regan, may have gone into the barn for a smoking break, then accidentally dropped a match into the dry hay. It was only after struggling unsuccessfully to stamp out the fire that he ran from the barn to wake the O'Leary family. Two days later, realizing he was responsible for starting one of the greatest fires in the nation's history, he invented the story about sitting across the street as a cover.

The hypothesis of Richard Bales sparked the imagination of history enthusiasts across the nation. The *Chicago Tribune* and the *New York Times* published articles on his research, and he was invited to discuss his theory on news programs across America and overseas, including a detailed interview with the BBC. Best of all, based on his research, the Chicago city council passed a resolution that officially exonerated Mrs. O'Leary's cow of any criminal wrongdoing. As for the O'Leary house on DeKoven Street, it no longer exists. But in its place stands the Chicago Fire Academy, a school for the training of new firefighters. Marking the entrance to the academy is a 30-foot-high bronze sculpture made of three twisting flames. And where the barn once stood is a simple plaque that reads, "On this site stood the home and barn of Mrs. O'Leary's where the Chicago Fire of 1871 started. Although there are many versions of the story of its origin the real cause of the fire has never been determined."

Chronology

1803   Construction begins on Fort Dearborn, a government stockade and trading post, at the future site of Chicago.

1830   The state of Illinois lays out plans for two towns, Ottawa and Chicago, at the ends of a proposed canal connecting the Great Lakes–St. Lawrence and Mississippi River systems.

1833   The City of Chicago is founded after several American Indian tribes are coerced into giving their land to the U.S. government.

1848   The Illinois and Michigan Canal opens, and construction begins on Chicago's first railroad.

1857   Chicago becomes the center of the world's largest railroad network.

1871   **Saturday, October 7:** The Lull and Holmes fire begins at around 11 P.M. It burns for 17 hours and destroys 4 blocks in the West Side of the city.

Sunday, October 8

9:00 P.M.   The Great Chicago Fire begins in the barn of Patrick and Catherine O'Leary.

9:50 P.M.   The fire breaks through Taylor Street.

11:30 P.M.   The fire crosses the river to the South Side.

Monday, October 9

1:30 A.M.   The courthouse burns.

3:20 A.M.   The Waterworks burns, cutting off the firefighters' water supply.

Morning Refugees on the Sands are forced into Lake Michigan, where many wait until nightfall.

Tuesday, October 10

12:00 A.M. Rain begins to fall over the city.

6:00 P.M. Relief supplies begin rolling in from across the nation.

1873   The Panic of 1873 begins six years of nationwide economic depression, halting the initial, careless phase of reconstruction.

Timeline

Saturday, October 7
The Lull and Holmes Fire begins at around 11 P.M. It burns for 17 hours and destroys 4 blocks in the West Side of the city.

1871

Sunday, October 8
9:00 p.m.: The Great Chicago Fire begins in the barn of Patrick and Catherine O'Leary.
9:50 p.m.: The fire breaks through Taylor Street.
11:30 p.m.: The fire crosses the river to the South Side.

1879 The second phase of rebuilding begins. Over the next two decades, the Chicago School architects do their most important work.

1893 The city receives 27 million visitors, including 13 million from other countries, at the triumphant Chicago World's Fair.

Monday, October 9
1:30 a.m.: The courthouse burns.
3:20 a.m.: The Waterworks burns, cutting off the firefighters' water supply.
Morning: Refugees on the Sands are forced into Lake Michigan, where many wait until nightfall.

1871

Tuesday, October 10
12:00 a.m.: Rain begins to fall over the city.
6:00 p.m.: Relief supplies begin rolling in from across the nation.

Glossary

balloon frame   A framing structure marked by continuous studs.

behemoth   Enormous.

drayman   Cart driver.

ember   A hot ash that is the last glowing part of a fire.

fire devils   Superheated columns of air that rise with a twisting, tornado-like motion.

firestorm   A raging, intense fire that spreads quickly.

Gomorrah   In the Bible, one of two cities God punished for being full of sin.

impervious   Resistant.

industrialization   The introduction of a factory system and heavy manufacturing.

masonry   A structure built from brick or stone.

metropolis   A densely populated urban area.

pigsties   Pens for pigs.

typhoid   A highly infectious disease caused by contaminated drinking water.

Bibliography

Andreas, Alfred T. *History of Chicago from the Earliest Period to the Present Time, Volume II: From 1857 Until the Fire of 1871.* Chicago: A.T. Andreas Company, 1885.

Angle, Paul M., ed. *The Great Chicago Fire: Described in Seven Letters by Men and Women Who Experienced its Horrors.* Chicago: Chicago Historical Society, 1946.

Angle, Paul M., ed. *The Great Chicago Fire of 1871: Three Illustrated Accounts from Harper's Weekly.* Ashland, Ore.: Lewis Osborne, 1969.

Bales, Richard F. *The Great Chicago Fire and the Myth of Mrs. O'Leary's Cow.* Jefferson, N.C.: McFarland and Company, 2002.

Cromie, Robert. *The Great Chicago Fire.* New York: McGraw-Hill, 1958.

Cromie, Robert. *Short History of Chicago.* San Francisco: Lexikos, 1984.

Gess, Denise, and William Lutz. *Firestorm at Peshtigo.* New York: Henry Holt, 2002.

Kogan, Herman, and Robert Cromie. *The Great Fire.* New York: G.P. Putnam's Sons, 1971.

Lowe, David, ed. *The Great Chicago Fire in Eyewitness Accounts and 70 Contemporary Photographs and Illustrations.* New York: Dover Publications, 1979.

Masters, Edgar Lee. *The Tale of Chicago.* New York: G.P. Putnam's Sons, 1933.

Miller, Donald L. *City of the Century: The Epic of Chicago and the Making of America.* New York: Simon & Schuster, 1996.

Miller, Ross. *American Apocalypse: The Great Fire and the Myth of Chicago.* Chicago: University of Chicago Press, 1990.

Murphy, Jim. *The Great Fire.* New York: Scholastic, 1995.

Pauly, John J. "The Great Chicago Fire as a National Event." *American Quarterly* 36 (1984): 668–683.

Sawislak, Karen. *Smoldering City*. Chicago: University of Chicago Press, 1995.

Smith, Carl. *Urban Disorder and the Shape of Belief: The Great Chicago Fire, the Haymarket Bomb, and the Model Town of Pullman*. Chicago: University of Chicago Press, 1995.

Further Reading

BOOKS

The Great Fire by Jim Murphy. New York: Scholastic, 1995.

The Great Fire by Herman Kogan and Robert Cromie. New York: G.P. Putnam's Sons, 1971.

The Great Chicago Fire, 1871 by Elizabeth Massie (fiction). New York: Pocket Books, 1999.

Children of the Fire by Harriette Gillem Robinet (fiction). New York: Aladdin, 2001.

Firestorm at Peshtigo by Denise Gess and William Lutz. New York: Henry Holt, 2002.

WEB SITES

The Great Chicago Fire and the Web of Memory
http://www.chicagohs.org/fire/

Did the Cow Do It?
http://www.thechicagofire.com/

Chicago: City of the Century
http://www.pbs.org/wgbh/amex/chicago/index.html

Encyclopedia of Chicago
http://encyclopedia.chicagohistory.org/

The Peshtigo Fire
http://www.rootsweb.com/~wioconto/Fire.htm

Picture Credits

Index

About the Author

PAUL BENNIE holds writing degrees from Duke University and the Iowa Writer's Workshop. He lives in Iowa City, Iowa, where he works as a freelance writer and science editor.